Readings in Literary Criticism 8
CRITICS ON VIRGINIA WOOLF

Readings in Literary Criticism

Edited by
Judith O'Neill

In preparation

CRITICS ON
VIRGINIA WOOLF

Readings in Literary Criticism

Edited by Jacqueline E. M. Latham

University of Miami Press
Coral Gables, Florida

CONTENTS

INTRODUCTION

The six extracts at the beginning of this volume discuss Virginia Woolf's work in general terms and raise three important questions, the first of which is how far she was successful in portraying character. Discussion of this dates back at least to 1923 when Arnold Bennett wrote of *Jacob's Room*, her third novel: 'But the characters do not vitally survive in the mind because the author has been obsessed by details of originality and cleverness.' This judgment hurt Virginia Woolf, as her diary comment of July 19, 1923 shows, and she replied publicly in her delightfully imaginative though hard-hitting essay *Mr Bennett and Mrs Brown*. The controversy between the two novelists continued for several years, but in time familiarity with Virginia Woolf's methods led to greater understanding of her work and criticism took other forms, so that J. W. Beach, for example, deplored the narrowness of her range in excluding characters passionately committed in action and feeling.

Her prose style is the second important matter discussed in the introductory essays of this volume. M. C. Bradbrook, in her early *Scrutiny* article, criticizes some mannerisms of Virginia Woolf's style, but at the same time points out what many subsequent readers appear to have overlooked: her power as a satirist. More recently David Lodge has questioned David Daiches's well-known analysis of the devices used to represent the continuity of her characters' thoughts. But the chief study of those who have examined her language has been the imagery, particularly in the major novels where the central metaphors are supported by a close web of related images. It is from a close examination of these, for example the sea in *To the Lighthouse*, that some of the most valuable insights into the novels have been gained.

The significance of M. C. Bradbrook's article, however, does not lie in the observations about Virginia Woolf's prose style but in the charge that she avoids not only deep feelings but thought and even commitment to a moral viewpoint. This is the third question raised in these essays, and it is crucial, for Virginia Woolf's stature as a novelist depends very largely on whether we see her as a writer concerned only with creating a beautiful object or whether we can perceive a scheme of values, however personal, in her novels. The problem for the twentieth-century writer of how to communicate his own standards of moral judgment in a society which has no universally accepted system of values is discussed by Daiches in the first essay of this volume. Virginia Woolf herself envied the easy certainties of Jane Austen and Scott which freed them in a way she and her contemporaries could never share: 'To believe that your impressions hold good for others is to be released from the cramp and confinement of personality.' ('How it Strikes a Contemporary.') M. C. Bradbrook's criticism has been repeated by others associated with the so-called *Scrutiny* viewpoint, and F. R. Leavis, the editor of *Scrutiny*, expressed his opinion in a passage that has become famous:[1]

> The envelope enclosing her dramatized sensibilities may be 'semitransparent' but it seems to shut out all the ranges of experience accompanying those kinds of preoccupation, volitional and moral, with an external world which are not felt primarily as preoccupation with one's consciousness of it. The preoccupation with intimating 'significance' in fine shades of consciousness, together with the unremitting play of visual imagery, of 'beautiful' writing and the lack of moral interest and interest in action, give the effect of something closely akin to a sophisticated aestheticism.

The remaining essays in this volume discuss the novels in chronological order from *The Voyage Out*, published in 1915, to *Between the Acts*, published posthumously in 1941. By implication A. D. Moody and J. O'Brien Schaefer, among others, are providing an answer to the *Scrutiny* critics when they analyse individual novels, for they explore the discriminations made by Virginia Woolf and reveal the nature of the moral order to be found in her work. Moody, in his excellent little book, comes to this general conclusion:

> Her end is both to achieve an ordered wholeness in the individual life, and to project that order into the decadence and disintegration of her world; in short, to recreate her society and its culture in the image of the complete human person. The full meaning of her preoccupation with the inner life of the individual is that she sees that life to be inseparable from the life of society and civilization, and to be, moreover, its vital centre—both that which creates them and that which they exist to serve.

Kingston Polytechnic   *Jacqueline Latham*
Kingston-upon-Thames

[1] 'After *To the Lighthouse*', *Scrutiny*, Vol. 10, 1942.

ACKNOWLEDGEMENTS

We are grateful to the following for permission to use copyright material from the works whose titles follow in brackets:

The owners of *Accent* magazine (M. Brace's *Worshipping Solid Objects* and I. Gamble's *The Secret Sharer in* 'Mrs Dalloway'; we regret we have been unable to trace the authors themselves and would welcome any information which would enable us to do so); J. Bennett and Cambridge University Press (*Virginia Woolf: Her Art as a Novelist*); Professor M. C. Bradbrook and Cambridge University Press (*Notes on the Style of Mrs Woolf*); Professor D. Daiches and The University of Chicago Press (*The Novel and the Modern World*); Durham University Journal (C. Basham's 'Between the Acts'); Professor J. W. Graham and the University of Toronto Press (*Time in the Novels of Virginia Woolf* and *The 'Caricature Value' of Parody and Fantasy in* 'Orlando'); The Hogarth Press Ltd (Bernard Blackstone's *Virginia Woolf: A Commentary*); The Hogarth Press Ltd and Harcourt, Brace and World, Inc. (from *Virginia Woolf and Her Works*, copyright (c) 1962, by Jean Guiguet; translation (c) 1965 by the Hogarth Press. Reprinted by permission of Harcourt, Brace, Jovanovich, Inc.); David Lodge and Routledge and Kegan Paul Ltd (*The Language of Fiction*); Modern Fiction Studies (Marilyn Zorn's *The Pageant in* 'Between the Acts', *Modern Fiction Studies*, (c) 1956, by the Purdue Research Foundation, Lafayette, Indiana); Modern Language Association of America (John Hawley Roberts' '*Vision and Design*' *in Virginia Woolf*); New Directions (David Daiches' *Virginia Woolf*, copyright 1942, (c) 1963 by New Directions Publishing Corporation. Reprinted by permission of New Directions Publishing Corporation); Nigel Nicolson (V. Sackville-West's *Virginia Woolf and* 'Orlando'); Oliver and Boyd Ltd (A. D. Moody's *Virginia Woolf*); Josephine O'Brien Schaefer (*The Three-fold Nature of Reality in the Novels of Virginia Woolf*); Swets en Zeitlinger n.v. (Irene Simon's *Some Aspects of Virginia Woolf's Imagery*); The University of California Press (J. Hafley's *The Glass Roof*, reprinted by permission of The Regents of the University of California).

DAVID DAICHES

The Nature of Virginia Woolf's Art

In Virginia Woolf more than in any other English novelist the writer of
fiction faces squarely the problem of the breakdown of a public
sense of significance and its consequences for the novel. A novelist
who could ask, 'What is meant by reality?' and reply, 'It would seem
to be something very erratic, very undependable—now to be found in
a dusty road, now in a scrap of newspaper in the street, now in a
daffodil in the sun'; who specifically points out 'the power of their
belief' and the security of public conviction about fundamentals which
distinguish Scott and Jane Austen from her own contemporaries—such
a novelist does not have to wait for the critic to come along and explain
what she is doing and why she is doing it. She saw one aspect of the
modern problem with remarkable clarity, and consciously developed
a view of fictional art which would enable her to deal with it. Of course
she saw this not only as a modern problem but as a deep personal
need—the need to develop a kind of fiction which would render
persuasively the quality of her own personal insights into experience.
'Quality' is the word to use here, for Mrs Woolf was concerned less
with projecting any given view of what is significant in experience than
with the sort of thing, the moods, intuitions, blending of memories,
sudden awarenesses of the symbolic in the real, that suggests how the
inner life is really lived. The material environment, which she
criticized Bennett and Wells and Galsworthy for concentrating on,
was for her at most only a background, and even changes in status
and fortune (where they occur in her novels, which is rarely) are
shown as less interesting than the states of consciousness associated
with them. Even the change from life to death can be less significant
for her than the mutations of one person's consciousness into the
differing recollections of that person, and the differing responses to
the meaning of his or her personality, left in the consciousnesses of
others after he or she has died. Mrs Dalloway, reflecting on what
death might mean, speculates that perhaps in death she would become
'part of people she had never met; being laid out like a mist between
the people she knew best, who lifted her on their branches as she had
seen the trees lift the mist, but it spread ever so far, her life, herself.'
And in the last part of *To the Lighthouse* the dead Mrs Ramsay is
an important part of the texture of other consciousnesses.

It is true that in the rhythms of her prose, in the muted lilt of her
sentences with their repetitions and qualifications and subtle fading

from direct speech to brooding description and back again, Virginia Woolf sometimes provokes the reaction that it is all mere self-indulgent musing, an irresponsible playing about with life. But this is unjust. The novels are most carefully organized to present real patterns of meaning, and both characters and events are—by virtue of the way they are presented and of the part they play in the total pattern— endowed with symbolic significance that is much more than a mere sense of mood. Yet sense of mood is her starting point. The credibility of her best novels is established by the almost hypnotic force with which the author compels the reader to accept the mood she sets, with all its variations, as the novel flows on to its conclusion. Nothing could be further removed from Victorian fiction, in which the interest was maintained by public symbols, gain or loss of money, sudden fortune or sudden disgrace, or obvious emotional changes concerned with love or hate or hope or disappointment. The charge that Virginia Woolf's is an art of leisure, of unconcern with the practical affairs of daily life, is true but absurdly irrelevant. It might equally be made against the music of Mozart or the poems of Henry Vaughan. The important thing is that this delicate rendering of the different shades of experience, this subtle presentation of the texture of consciousness as it is woven by the individual's response to life, is made real and moving in Virginia Woolf's art. Whenever the claims of action are relaxed, when- ever the pressure of external events is dropped so as to allow room for that leisure of the sensibilities in which the self can relish the meaning of its own responses and its own history, then Mrs Woolf's world comes into existence. Perhaps the greatest fictional art weaves together the world of action and the world of introspection, the sense of the dailiness of daily living and the moods of private illumination which illumine and even transfigure routine; Virginia Woolf at her best restricts herself to certain kinds of response made possible in certain kinds of situation. She limited herself to this because it was this that interested her most and challenged her to produce her finest art. If we agree that her finest and most characteristic novels make their appeal to that twilight mood of receptive reverie (inducing that mood in the reader in order to appeal to it), if they steer us toward a new kind of knowledge through the rendering of almost familiar moods where we feel a deep sense of recognition and acquiescence and at the same time a sense of wonder and surprise; if they give us a general sense of meaning and relevance even before we have discovered what the meaning and relevance really are, that is all part of the intention. That, for Virginia Woolf, is how significance manifests itself in experience; she shows us her world of values in action, and in doing so makes use of our tendency to reverie—which is not the same as reducing all life to reverie. Thus while Joyce solves the problem of selection and significance by finding devices to enable him to show everything as simultaneously both significant and insignificant,

Virginia Woolf, operating by restriction rather than by expansion, solves it by winning the co-operation of the reader's ordinary human tendency to reverie in order to present and to make convincing through a texture largely of reverie her own personal sense of significance. It may be true that she does not succeed in making her view convincing to all readers. A novelist who works by restriction in this way always risks limiting his appeal. But there will always be readers to whom her best and most characteristic novels will evoke that combination of recognition and discovery which only novels of real quality and originality can produce.

It is the texture of Virginia Woolf's novels which holds the reader, and the structure which determines the symbolic meanings of each phase of the action. This division of labour is more deliberate than it is in most novelists; in a sense it is artificial; but all art is artificial, and it is a matter of degree and of the convention within which an artist works. The large canvas, with its exuberant colour and caricature, carrying the meaning along with careless splendour, is not Mrs Woolf's way, though it is a way very deeply entrenched in the English literary tradition. Some readers resent having to hunt for the total meaning of a novel as they have to do for the meaning of a metaphysical poem. But this means that they have not been captured by the initial appeal of the texture, and if they have not there is nothing more to be said. To this extent Virginia Woolf is a minor novelist; one's response to her novels will depend in the last analysis on one's temperament. . . .

From Chapter 10 of *The Novel and the Modern World*, revised edition, University of Chicago Press, Chicago, 1960, pp. 187–191.

Her Characters' Limitations

... The Edwardians she found at fault in supposing that the ego is constituted by material things—houses, servants, fathers, incomes. She makes the mistake herself of supposing that the ego is constituted by the imaginative impressions that snow down upon it like cosmic rays. 'Let us record the atoms as they fall upon the mind.'

Now, I do not question the importance in shaping the personalities of the atoms that fall upon the mind. But we cannot stop there. We cannot suppose that every one of the myriad atoms so falling on the mind makes a distinct impression on the personality, or that the mind on which they fall is utterly passive to them. An utterly passive mind would receive no impression at all from the falling atoms. There is in every mind some principle of selection, some agency of choice. And this agency of choice is in the character—that is, in the attitudes and emotions of the person concerned. And what defines the attitudes and emotions? Why, the objectives, the ends sought, and the line of action that promises to realize these ends. The psychologist, I think, would tell us that character is determined by the organization of energies for action. The senses and the mind are instruments of behaviour. It is not, then, things in themselves that constitute character, nor is it the passive reception of impressions. It is the manner of organization of human energy for behaviour. The stream of consciousness is indeed an important factor in human experience, but subjection to the stream of consciousness is the sign of a weak and ill-defined character. A notable subjection to it is an indication of some dissolution of the psyche, some morbid want of continuity between conception and execution. The strong character is one that, among the multifarious 'atoms' of the stream of consciousness, centres its attention on those that are most relevant to its objectives.

In fiction there is nothing that makes more for vividness of character than strong desire met by strong resistance in the person himself or in the circumstances encountered. This is the principle of tragic drama, in which the tension is created by the strength of a will pitted against the strength of circumstance. There is a similar tension in all stories where the moral sense is shown offering its resistance to the character's desire. In comedy, the interest lies in a sharp contrast between the character's pretensions and his real motives, or between the triviality of his performance and the lofty standard against which it is measured. In Mrs Woolf there is no tincture of tragedy and only the faintest hint of comedy. She is too 'modern' for melodrama or morality. Everything is bathed in a solution of sympathy and understanding. This may be a fine thing in its own way, as is the mystical dream of life in its flow. But it does not make for differentiation of character, nor for either the gusty sense of life in action or the sense of coming to grips with life.

Mrs Woolf's characters seldom seem to know what they want with any definiteness, nor want it with passion.[1] Some are supposed to be earning their livings or pursuing careers. But we are never shown what it means to earn a living, never made to feel the pinch of need, the lure of the game, still less the 'rigour of the game'. They are said to fall in love, but it is like people in a dream; there is no hint of a biological urge or even of the passion of the ego. They marry people of their own class rather than those they love, but there is little suggestion of the agony of unsatisfied love or the frightful ennui of a life of convenience. We are told that Clarissa took hard her break with Peter, that she 'had borne about with her for years like an arrow sticking in her heart the grief, the anguish'. But this is shockingly out of key with the rest of the picture; we don't know whether to take it as the author's sober view of the case or the effusive tone of a sentimental society woman. In general, Mrs Woolf does not seem to realize the tragic intensity with which human beings take their ambitions, their disappointments, their very boredoms. . . .

If there is one thing that Mrs Woolf loves more than another, it is unfinished sentences, fragmentary conversations, questions unanswered and unformulated. These correspond to lines of conduct vaguely projected and early broken off. It is such things that give their special character of futility to the lives of the Pargiters and their friends in *The Years*. They are eminently 'nice' people; but they need nothing, want nothing, and get nowhere either in their lives or in their thinking. There seems to be some realization on the author's part that this is so, and she has introduced certain characters for the express purpose of passing judgment on these people. They dream of a way of acting 'differently' from those who came before them, but the difference they envisage is so vague, so 'spiritual'—in short, so sentimental—that it gives away the game. Neither North nor Peggy nor, seemingly, the author has any notion that it is the decadence of a social order which they are witnessing, and that a willingness to act in a material world is the necessary preliminary to any real spiritual regeneration.

[1] For me the most convincing of her character-creations is Mr Ramsay in *To the Lighthouse*, and the most interesting situation is that involving him and his son and daughter while on their sailing trip. I wish there were space to analyse the character of Mr Ramsay and show how its vividness derives from the force of this man's need for a woman's sympathy, and how the intensity of the relation between him and his son grows out of their sharply defined rivalry for a woman's affection.

There is no evidence through all her work that Mrs Woolf has a comprehension of the social forces underlying the world she describes. And I cannot but feel that there is an element of sentimental evasion in her inveterate preference—at least in fiction—for vagueness of feeling and thought. She has given an excellent representation of the surface psychology of well-meaning and sensitive people floating without effort on the surface of a social order designed to give them ease and security. These people are legion; and large numbers of them, no doubt, are mainly characterized by the sort of daydreaming which we have in Clarissa and Mrs Ramsay and Lily Briscoe and Bernard; so we must acknowledge that she has added something considerable to our aesthetic satisfaction in thus delineating a significant type of human nature. But it is not the most interesting type for fiction, not being strong enough to move us deeply. And her characters of this type are not sufficiently individualized—as to sex, for example, and special predicament—to make a truly 'dramatic' offering. Her leading characters are so like in idiom and tone of mind that one is tempted to regard them as little more than variations on a single theme, and this theme drawn from something in the author's own temperament. If that is right, what we have is, properly speaking, a series of lyrical utterances in story form. They are an authentic document in psychology. They are highly interesting in method and manner. And they make up altogether a distinctive and original contribution to the store of English fiction.

From 'Virginia Woolf', *The English Journal*, Vol. 26, 1937, pp. 603–12 (608–12). (The page numbers before the bracket give the beginning and end of the whole article; those within the bracket the pages of the actual extract.)

JOAN BENNETT

Characters and Human Beings

Mr E. M. Forster[1] writes of Virginia Woolf

> she could seldom so portray a character that it was remembered afterwards on its own account, as Emma is remembered, for instance, or Dorothea Casaubon, or Sophia and Constance in *The Old Wives' Tale*.

Nor is Mr Forster alone in feeling that Virginia Woolf's mature novels fail to provide a gallery of memorable portraits, such as can be derived from the works of other great novelists. However that may be, it is certain that she developed a different method of characterization from theirs, and one that produces a different effect. In her first two books some, but not all, of the characters are first introduced in the traditional way. Mr Hilbery, who plays a minor role in *Night and Day*, is sketched for the reader at his first appearance:

> He was an elderly man, with a pair of oval, hazel eyes which were rather bright for his time of life, and relieved the heaviness of his face. He played constantly with a little green stone attached to his watch chain, thus displaying long and very sensitive fingers, and had a habit of moving his head hither and thither very quickly without altering the position of his large and rather corpulent body, so that he seemed to be providing himself incessantly with food for amusement and reflection with the least possible expenditure of energy. One might suppose that he had passed the time of life when his ambitions were personal, or that he had gratified them as far as he was likely to do, and now employed his considerable acuteness rather to observe and reflect than to attain any result.

The fault here is a slight overloading with detail, and the physical traits are made to carry an undue burden of psychological significance, a common fault with this type of presentation. The essential characteristics of an outline portrait are there, the key to the character is given, Mr Hilbery is an individual not merely a type, his main characteristics are easily remembered and can be developed and confirmed by his subsequent behaviour, thus giving the reader the self-gratulatory feeling of having understood him from the first. . . . But the presentation of Rachel, in *The Voyage Out*, and of Katharine Hilbery, in *Night and Day*, is of a different kind; the reader discovers

[1] *Virginia Woolf*, by E. M. Forster, Cambridge University Press, 1942.

B

them gradually and incompletely, in part from their own speech and reflections, in part from their effect upon other people. They are more elusive than Mr Hilbery . . . just as, in real life, the people we know intimately are more elusive than our acquaintance—we are aware that there is always something more to be discovered. The first picture we have of Rachel is a picture in the mind of Helen Ambrose:

> Helen looked at her. Her face was weak rather than decided, saved from insipidity by the large enquiring eyes; denied beauty, now that she was sheltered indoors, by the lack of colour and definite outline. Moreover, a hesitation in speaking, or rather a tendency to use the wrong words, made her seem more than normally incompetent for her years. Mrs Ambrose, who had been speaking much at random, now reflected that she certainly did not look forward to the intimacy of three or four weeks on board ship which was threatened. Women of her own age usually boring her, she supposed that girls would be worse. She glanced at Rachel again. Yes! how clear it was that she would be vacillating, emotional, and when you said something to her it would make no more lasting impression than the stroke of a stick upon water. There was nothing to take hold of in girls—nothing hard, permanent, satisfactory.

But the book, instead of developing and confirming this impression, contradicts it at many points; Helen has not taken the place of an omniscient narrator and given the reader a clue to Rachel's character; she has revealed a little of herself and of the first impression Rachel makes on a critical observer, but no more. Katharine in *Night and Day* is introduced as Denham first sees her, and there also we are not given the illusion that the picture is complete, nor even necessarily correct. Even in these first two books the people who most interest the reader cannot be summed up. When Mary Datchet attempts to find a label for Katharine, the reader is left in no doubt of its inadequacy:

> Mary felt herself baffled, and put back again into the position in which she had been at the beginning of their talk. It seemed to her that Katharine possessed a curious power of drawing near and receding, which sent alternate emotions through her far more quickly than was usual, and kept her in a condition of curious alertness. Desiring to classify her, Mary bethought her of the convenient term 'egoist'.
>
> 'She's an egoist,' she said to herself, and stored that word up to give to Ralph one day when, as it would certainly fall out, they were discussing Miss Hilbery.

The irrelevance of the classifying word is obvious both in its immediate context and in relation to the rest of our knowledge of Katharine. The word 'egoist' tells us little about Katharine, but it expresses a need of Mary's, the need to define her and so be able to control her own reactions to Katharine's dynamic personality. She can only do this by holding her at a distance and so getting her as it were into focus. Virginia Woolf came to believe that all definition of character involved such a refusal to come near and that *character* in the sense in which the word is used of persons in fiction, or, as often as not in biography, does not exist in real life. It is possible that the impression that she does not create clear or memorable characters is due to the fact that her portraits are of a different kind from those to which the reader of fiction is accustomed. . . .

After 1919 the aspects of life in which Virginia Woolf could believe with conviction ceased to include the clearly definable human character. The people in her later books frequently express her own unwillingness to circumscribe human beings within the compass of a *character*. Mrs Dalloway, for instance:

> She would not say of anyone in the world now that they were this or that.

Or Mrs Ramsay, reflecting on the nature of the self:

> . . . one after another, she, Lily, Augustus Carmichael, must feel, our apparitions, the things you know us by, are simply childish. Beneath it is all dark, it is all spreading, it is unfathomably deep; but now and again we rise to the surface and that is what you see us by.

When Virginia Woolf became fully conscious that the traditional method of characterization could not interpret her own vision of human beings, she sought for other means of communicating it. *Jacob's Room* is the first of her novels which wholly rejects the old method; but in it her new technique is not yet used with the ease and assurance she was later to acquire. Jacob Flanders is never directly described, and he rarely reveals himself to the reader by what he says or does. Instead we derive our impression of him from the effect he produces on other people in the novel. . . .

From the conviction expressed [in *Jacob's Room*, pp. 70–1] about the incompleteness of our knowledge of one another; and from the certainty . . . communicated that our fellow-beings do nevertheless arouse in us profound and valued feelings, springs Virginia Woolf's individual art of creating human beings. The method is cumulative, and it is therefore impossible to isolate from her books a portrait which epitomizes a particular character, either by means of description or dramatization. Nevertheless, it seems to me false to suggest, as Mr Forster does, that the beings she creates are less memorable than the persons in other great works of fiction. Mrs Ramsay, Mrs Dalloway, Eleanor Pargiter, each of the main personalities in *Between the Acts*, and many others from her books, inhabit the mind of the reader and enlarge the capacity for imaginative sympathy. It is sympathy rather than judgment that she invokes, her personages are apprehended rather than comprehended. Increasingly the writer eliminates herself from her books, the illusion of the all-seeing eye is replaced by the illusion that we are seeing by glimpses, with our own imperfect vision. Far more, however, is set before our eyes in the books than in normal experience. . . .

From Chapter 2 of *Virginia Woolf: Her Art as a Novelist,* Cambridge University Press, Cambridge, 1964, pp. 19–27.

M. C. BRADBROOK

Notes on the Style of Mrs Woolf

In reading any of the later novels of Mrs Woolf, a curious and persistent trick of style obtrudes itself on the attention.

> But for women, I thought, looking at the empty shelves, these difficulties are infinitely more formidable. . . .
> The mind is certainly a very mysterious organ, I reflected, drawing in my head from the window, about which practically nothing is known. . . .
> There is a coherence in things, a stability: something, she meant, is immune from change and shines out (she glanced at the window with its ripple of reflected light). Here, she felt, putting down the spoon, here was the still space that lies about the heart of things. . . .

The first two passages are ratiocinative, the last a description of a mood. Yet the little asides serve the same purpose in all three: by stressing time and place, they deflate the statement: the affirmation is given a relative value only: neither the reader nor the writer is implicated: they are not trapped into any admissions, or required to endorse anything in more than a qualified way. The effect has been described by T. E. Hulme:

> The classical poet never forgets the finiteness, the limit of man. . . .
> If you say an extravagant thing, there is always the impression of yourself standing outside it and not quite believing it.

Mrs Woolf refuses to be pinned down in this way, and consequently she is debarred from a narrative technique, since this implies a schema of values, or even from the direct presentation of powerful feelings or major situations. In *Mrs Dalloway* the most powerful feelings depend on more powerful feelings long past: the old relationships between Clarissa, Peter, and Sally Seton, the war experiences of Septimus Warren Smith. They are reflected, indirect, 'the reward of having cared for people . . .'. In *To the Lighthouse* the feelings are peripheral: they are minor manifestations of powerful forces: as for instance when Mrs Ramsay reassures her husband on the terrace. The success of the book is due to the fact that the reader accepts the implication of the major forces behind the small situations. But even then the real nature of the subject is cloaked by Mrs Woolf's method of description through a kind of metaphor which has a highly abstracting effect.

Whenever the direct presentation of powerful feelings or major situations is inescapable, Mrs Woolf takes refuge in an embarrassing kind of nervous irony (as in the bracketed passages in *To the Lighthouse*, Part Two):

> This violent kind of disillusionment is usually to be expected of young men in the prime of life, sound in wind and limb, who will later become fathers of families and directors of banks.
> Here a girl for sale: there an old woman with only matches to offer.
> A shell exploded. Twenty or thirty young men were blown up in France, among them Andrew Ramsay, whose death, mercifully, was instantaneous.

That 'mercifully' at least might have been spared.

For Doris Kilman and Charles Tansley (who are parallel figures) Mrs Woolf reserves her heaviest satire. Miss Kilman's feelings for Elizabeth or Tansley's sensations at the dinner party are analysed with a brutality that is faintly discomforting. They are both devoid of the social sense, scholars who have developed the intelligence at the expense of the arts of living.

The heroines on the contrary live by their social sense: they are peculiarly sensitive to tone and atmosphere: they are in fact artists in the social medium, with other people's temperaments and moods as their materials. Mrs Ramsay is the complement of Lily Briscoe, 'Mrs Ramsay, saying *Life stand still here*: Mrs Ramsay making of the moment something permanent (as in another sphere Lily herself tried to make of the moment something permanent). . . . In the midst of chaos there was shape: this eternal passing and flowing was struck into stability. *Life stand still here*, Mrs Ramsay said.'

It is the arresting of a single 'moment', a significant spot in the temporal sequence that is Art for Mrs Ramsay and Mrs Woolf. In *The Spot on the Wall*, Mrs Woolf describes her technique, which is essentially static. A single moment is isolated and forms a unit for the sensibility to work on. The difficulty lies in relating the various moments. Intensity is the only criterion of a detached experience and there is a consequent tendency for everything to be equally intense in Mrs Woolf's works. Everything receives the same slightly strained attention: the effect is not unlike that of tempera painting, where there is exquisite delicacy of colour, but no light and shade. (The connection of this with the refusal to assent to a statement absolutely is too obvious to need any stressing.)

Mrs Woolf's difficulties have always been structural. In *Jacob's Room* she hardly attempted a solution: in *Mrs Dalloway* she began the rigid telescoping of the time sequence which was developed in *To the Lighthouse*. A series of echoes and cross references form the real framework of the book; they are of the kind Joyce had used in

Ulysses, but there is nothing to correspond to the more bony support which in *Ulysses* is provided by the structure of the episodes. The precarious stability of *To the Lighthouse* dissolved into the muddle of *Orlando* (in any case a *jeu d'esprit*), and the futile counterpointing of *The Waves.*

Mrs Woolf's books seem to be built up in a mosaic from the 'moments': scenes, descriptions, odd names recur from time to time. Here is a typical case:

> Already the convolvulus moth was spinning over the flowers. Orange and purple, nasturtium and cherry pie, were washed into the twilight but the tobacco plant and the passion flower over which the great moths spun were white as china. . . .
> How she loved the grey white moths spinning in and out, over the cherry pie, over the evening primroses.

Moll Pratt the flowerseller and the Reverend Edward Whittaker, figures who appear for a moment only, are in *Jacob's Room* and *Mrs Dalloway;* and the Dalloways themselves are of course from *The Voyage Out.*

This kind of thing developed into the subtler correspondence between Parts One and Three of *To the Lighthouse* as, for instance, Cam's recollections of the stag's head.

The significant moments, the units of Mrs Woolf's style are either delicate records of the external scene, expressed in epigrammatic metaphor usually ('The whole platefuls of blue sea', 'The dragon-fly paused and then shot its blue stitch further through the air') or the presentation of a mood such as Mrs Ramsay's reverie on the terrace. These moods are hardly ever dramatic, i.e. bound by the limitations of the character who experiences them. The personality of Mrs Ramsay on the terrace or of Mrs Dalloway in her drawing room does not matter: neither their individuality nor the plot is of any relevance. The mood is in fact an isolated piece of pure recording, of a more complex kind but not essentially different from the epigrammatic metaphor. It is less an emotion than a sensation that is presented: the feeling is further depersonalized by Mrs Woolf's use of metaphor: for instance in the description of Mr Ramsay appealing to his wife.

These two elements of Mrs Woolf's style, the observation of the external world and the description of moods, are separated out in her last book, *The Waves.* The interchapters describe the movements of sun and tides (the sea is for Mrs Woolf a symbol of the eternal and indifferent natural forces): this movement forms a kind of parallel to the development of the lives of the characters. But the effect of a page or two of epigrammatic metaphor is very fatiguing: the myopic observation, the lack of variations in the tension impose a strain on the reader. Sometimes phrase-making conquers accuracy: 'the lark peeled his clear ring of song and dropped it through the silent air' suggests the long call of a blackbird, but hardly the trills and twitters of the lark.

In the main portion of the book, there are no solid characters, no clearly defined situations and no structure of feelings: merely sensation in the void. Without any connections of a vital sort between them, with no plot in the Aristotelian sense, the sensations are not interesting. Emotions are reduced to a description of their physical accompaniments: the attention is wholly peripheral. This for example is the equivalent of the experience of being in love:

> Then there is the being drawn out, eviscerated, spun like a spider's web, twisted in agony round a thorn: then a thunder clap of complete indifference: the light blown out: then the return of measureless inexpressible joy: certain fields seemed to glow green for ever.

There had been hints of this danger even in the earlier works: 'how could one express in words these emotions of the body? To want and not to have, sent up all her body a hardness, a hollowness, a strain.' Physical sensations, which are immediately present, and have no relations to any schema of values, are all that Mrs Woolf dares to assume in her readers.

All attempt to order and select has gone. 'There is nothing that one can fish up with a spoon, nothing that one can call an event. . . . How impossible to order them rightly, to detach one separately or give the effect of the whole. . . . Nevertheless, life is pleasant, life is tolerable. Monday is followed by Tuesday, then comes Wednesday.'

Mrs Woolf never, as is so frequently asserted, attempts to reproduce the process of thinking. Such generalized activity does not interest her: moreover, thinking implies a thesis which one is ready to defend. Mr Ramsay, who is a philosopher, 'thinks' with the most helpless particularity: the progress of human thought is symbolized for him by an alphabet, just as for Lily Briscoe, a large kitchen table stands for the mental pursuits of Mr Ramsay himself. Their mental atmospheres are indistinguishable: and in both cases, the mood is not one of thought but of reverie.

The heroines are astonishingly ingenuous. Their tact and sensitiveness are preserved in a kind of intellectual vacuum. Mrs Dalloway 'muddled Armenians and Turks: and to this day, ask her what the Equator was and she did not know.' Mrs Ramsay ponders 'A square root? What was that? Her sons knew. She leant on them: on cubes and square roots: that was what they were talking about . . . and the French system of land tenure. . . . She let it uphold her, this admirable fabric of the masculine intelligence.' Compare the dependence of Mrs Flanders and even of Lady Bruton.

The camouflage in A Room of One's Own serves the same purpose as this nervous particularizing: it prevents Mrs Woolf from committing the indelicacy of putting a case or the possibility of her being accused of waving any kind of banner. The arguments are clearly serious and personal and yet they are dramatized and surrounded with all sorts of disguises to avoid an appearance of argument.

The shrinking of the heroines is too conscious as the playfulness of *A Room of One's Own* is too laboured. To demand 'thinking' from Mrs Woolf is clearly illegitimate: but such a deliberate repudiation of it and such a smoke screen of feminine charm is surely to be deprecated. Mrs Woolf has preserved her extraordinary fineness and delicacy of perception at the cost of some cerebral etiolation.

From 'Notes on the Style of Mrs Woolf', *Scrutiny*, Vol. 1, 1932, pp. 33–8. The footnote page references to Virginia Woolf's novels have been omitted.

DAVID LODGE

Some Verbal Features of
Virginia Woolf's Novels

...Professor David Daiches[1] has called attention to the function of certain recurrent verbal features of Virginia Woolf's novels. (1) Her use of the third person pronoun, *one* ('it was not her one hated, but the idea of her'), as a way of indicating a certain agreement on the part of the writer with a character's thoughts. (2) Her use of *for* to link different stages of association in a character's stream of consciousness ('To dance, to ride, she had adored all that. [New para.] For they might be parted for hundreds of years, she and Peter'), *for* being 'a word which does not indicate a strict logical sequence ... but does suggest a relationship which is at least half-logical'. (3) Her persistent use of present participles of action ('Such fools, we are, she thought, crossing Victoria Street') 'to allow the author to remind the reader of the character's position, without interrupting the thought stream'.

There is no doubt that these are significant expressive features of Virginia Woolf's work, or that they have the effects described by Daiches. But one could go further and make the following points: (1) The use of the pronoun *one* is a characteristic upper-middle-class speech habit which, while it appears to withdraw modestly from crude assertion, slyly invokes authority from some undefined community of feeling and prejudice, into which it seeks to draw the auditor. Has Virginia Woolf entirely resolved her own attitude to characters like Mrs Dalloway, and is she entirely open about the degree of indulgence she expects the reader to extend to them? (2) The use of *for* to suggest logical connection where none exists might reveal a certain timidity in exploring the flow of consciousness and a disposition to simplify its workings. (3) The verb-participle construction establishes a divorce between cerebration and physical action which is not as normative as Virginia Woolf's fiction implies. We do not always think of eternity while serving potatoes; sometimes we just think of serving potatoes. Virginia Woolf's characters never do.

In other words, the devices brought forward by Daiches to illustrate Virginia Woolf's expressive use of language, while they certainly help

---

[1] David Daiches, *Virginia Woolf*, 1942, pp. 64-5 and 71-3. The illustrations are from *Mrs Dalloway*.

to explain how her presentation of experience gets its special character, might be used as evidence for alleging certain important limitations in her art. In this event, the very frequency of occurrence which makes these devices significant would be seen as damaging, contributing to an overall effect of monotonous sameness in the presentation of consciousnesses whose unique constitutions should be reflected in the language (as for instance in the comparable fiction of Joyce). . . .

From Chapter 3 of *The Language of Fiction*, Routledge and Kegan Paul, London, 1966, pp. 85–6.

JOHN GRAHAM

Time in the Novels of
Virginia Woolf

Virginia Woolf adhered to her own critical dictum, expressed most fully in *Mr Bennett and Mrs Brown,* that the business of the novelist is the exploration of character. The final goal of such exploration, however, is insight into the nature of human personality, and so into the meaning of life: for Mrs Brown, whose character is the proper subject of the novel, is really 'the spirit we live by, life itself'. In struggling to reach the goal, Mrs Woolf is constantly preoccupied with problems relating to time, as most critics have noted. This preoccupation underlies her concern with the phenomena of memory, change, and death, and drives her to ask several ancient difficult questions. Her efforts to answer them result in two central views of life, neither of which is the result of mere neurotic nescience.

I

In the first three novels—*The Voyage Out, Night and Day,* and *Jacob's Room*—the questions are asked in a fairly obvious way, and focus on the apparent dichotomy between two kinds of time, two worlds: on the one hand, the world of linear time, of past, present, and future, in which we are subject to unremittent and uncontrollable flux; and on the other hand, the world of mind time, an inner world of thought and imagination, in which the chaotic flow of experience derived from our life in linear time is reduced to order and unity, and in which we are therefore liberated. In all of her novels, Mrs Woolf is troubled by the apparent dualistic conflict between these two worlds, in which the data of one frequently contradict the data of the other; but she is never willing to accept this dualism as absolute. In seeking to overcome it, two solutions are possible: either both worlds are parts of one larger reality, and are therefore integrally related to each other; or one of these worlds is unreal, and only in exploring the other shall we find a valid absolute.

In the first three novels neither of these solutions is worked out: the problem is stated, not solved. These novels are dominated by what is called in one of them 'the profound and reasonless law' of linear time.[1] In this immense machine, human life is irrelevant; and against its tyranny the inner world of mind time opposes at best an escape into illusion. But in her next novel, Mrs Woolf does offer a solution, which depends to a great extent on the relationship between Clarissa Dalloway and Septimus Smith.

Although Clarissa exults in the 'triumph and the jingle' of 'life; London; this moment of June' (p. 6), she is also afflicted by a sense of isolation and by the recurring terror of death. The nature of her predicament is expressed most powerfully when she stands in a little room, watching the old lady in the house across the way:

Big Ben struck the half hour.

How extraordinary it was, strange, yes, touching, to see the old lady (they had been neighbours ever so many years) move away from that window, as if she were attached to that sound, that string. Gigantic as it was, it had something to do with her. Down, down, into the midst of ordinary things the finger fell making the moment solemn. She was forced, so Clarissa imagined, by that sound, to move, to go—but where? ... Why creeds and prayers and mackintoshes? when, thought Clarissa, that's the miracle, that's the mystery; that old lady, she meant, whom she could see going from chest of drawers to dressing-table. She could still see her. And the supreme mystery which Kilman might say she had solved, or Peter might say he had solved, but Clarissa didn't believe either of them had the ghost of an idea of solving, was simply this: here was one room, there another. Did religion solve that, or love? (pp. 140–1).

In many of Mrs Woolf's novels—as, for example, in *Jacob's Room*—the room symbolizes the selfhood formed in time. From her small room, then, Clarissa looks out and sees the supreme mystery: that people exist in the same stream of time, each moving under the compulsion of the time-flow (as symbolized by Big Ben), visible to each other, yet unknown to each other and essentially alone. Not even the great unifying forces of love and religion can supply any pattern relating them to each other. Clarissa tentatively theorizes about the unifying power of human personality, the 'unseen part of us, which spreads wide' (p. 168), and which persists after death, relating the individual to the dead and the absent, and to all that they have known. But this nebulous hope, held uncertainly, is clarified into a positive conviction only by the life and death of Septimus Smith.

In considering Septimus, we should remember what Mrs Woolf said in the preface: first, he was not included in the first draft of the novel; second, Clarissa was to die or commit suicide in the first draft; and third, Septimus is the 'double' of Clarissa.

[1] *The Voyage Out*, p. 322. [In this and subsequent essays all page references are to the Uniform Edition of Virginia Woolf's works published by the Hogarth Press].

'It might be possible, Septimus thought, looking at England from the train window, as they left Newhaven; it might be possible that the world itself is without meaning' (p. 98). With this thought begins his purgatorial voyage into insanity. Eventually he surrenders to his madness, seeking in no way to preserve any connection with humanity as it is directed in the ringing grooves of change by Doctors Holmes and Bradshaw. At this low point of his negative way into darkness Septimus receives his revelations. Sitting in Regent Park, he looks at the trees: 'But they beckoned; leaves were alive; trees were alive. And the leaves being connected by millions of fibres with his own body, there on the seat, fanned it up and down; when the branch stretched he, too, made the statement. The sparrows fluttering, rising, and falling in jagged fountains were part of the pattern; the white and blue, barred with black branches. Sounds made harmonies with premeditation; the spaces between them were as significant as the sounds. A child cried. Rightly far away a horn sounded. All taken together meant the birth of a new religion' (p. 26).

Septimus now sees, first, that there is a unifying reality hidden in the phenomena of time which gives them pattern and significance, and second, that the pattern is eternal because there is no death. These are revelations which, if he could communicate them to mankind, would save us, for he comes as a saviour, a redeemer: 'Look, the unseen bade him, the voice which now communicated with him who was the greatest of mankind, Septimus, lately taken from life to death, the Lord who had come to renew society, who lay like a coverlet, a snow blanket smitten only by the sun, for ever unwasted, suffering for ever, the scapegoat, the eternal sufferer. . . .' (p. 29). The ancient image of the sun, symbolizing the power of divine revelation; the image of the Saviour; the emphasis upon the fact that he was lately taken from life (the life of self, the life in time) to death (the annihilation of self, the transcendence of time): all suggest that Septimus has had the vision of a cosmic unity which Clarissa, rooted as she is in the process of time, can receive only dimly and briefly. Her moment of vision, characteristically derived from her response to a human emotion, is described as 'a match burning in a crocus; an inner meaning almost expressed' (p. 36); but the illumination is for Septimus as agonizingly blinding as the blaze of a fiercely intense sun. He is a snow blanket smitten only by the sun; or again, he is a figure, lamenting the fate of man in the desert alone, who receives full on his face the light of the dawning sun, an 'astonishing revelation' (p. 78).

There is, however, a fatal and ironic flaw in the vision of Septimus: it is more than flesh can endure. His descent into the pit is naturally marked by agonized suffering; but even the saving revelations beat upon him with merciless intensity. The true terror of his vision is that it destroys him as a creature of the time-world. When he returns for a brief tranquil period to the world of actuality, it would seem that this is not so. He feels that Nature is redeemed for him by his vision; and certainly Rezia is redeemed through her love. The world is no longer without meaning, he feels: time is a garment of eternity now, a coverlet of flowers (p. 157).

But Septimus does not really return to sanity—the appalling sanity of Holmes and Bradshaw, our fallen selves. He has died to that sanity and cannot effect any Lazarean return. He is no longer human, and can only rise up from death to another level of being, after walking briefly in a world of flowers. Holmes and Bradshaw must crucify him: they seek dominion through the body (both are doctors), and their understanding is of the body. Therefore, when they finally return to kill him (as he believes), he cries, 'I'll give it you!' and with a dreadful casualness, which makes Holmes and the fallen reader turn pale, he leaps towards the central spiritual reality, leaving for them their due legacy—a piece of dead flesh, pierced and torn.

These points must be made in order to grasp the full significance of the relationship between Septimus and Clarissa. This relationship is progressively revealed in the long scene after she hears of his death and walks alone into the little room from which, earlier in the day, she had watched the old lady across the way. There she reflects on his death:

> She had once thrown a shilling into the Serpentine, never any-
> thing more. But he had flung it away. They went on living (she
> would have to go back; the rooms were still crowded; people kept
> on coming). They (all day she had been thinking of Bourton, of
> Peter, of Sally), they would grow old. A thing there was that
> mattered; a thing, wreathed about with chatter, defaced, obscured
> in her own life, let drop every day in corruption, lies, chatter. This
> he had preserved. Death was defiance. Death was an attempt to
> communicate; people feeling the impossibility of reaching the centre
> which, mystically, evaded them; closeness drew apart; rapture
> faded, one was alone. There was an embrace in death (p. 202).

The meaning of Septimus' suicide is reinforced by the fact that he dies by leaping through a window. The window is used constantly as a symbol of the outlook of the self on the world around it. For the ordinary individual it is the aperture through which comes the only light he may receive; but it is also a barrier, hampering any movement of his being towards the source of that light. Clarissa makes no effort to break the pane of glass standing between herself and the sun; Septimus does: he casts off his temporal selfhood and leaps towards the centre. Clarissa realizes that in his act is an integrity which she can never have entire, rooted as she is in time: for, as we have seen, in order to penetrate to the centre, like Septimus, one must either die, or go mad, or in some other way lose one's humanity in order to exist independently of time.

Clarissa, then, accepts actuality: she even invites Bradshaw to her party. And it is Clarissa who enters the room at the end of the book and triumphs over time. Septimus cannot triumph, but his is the complete vision which gives Clarissa the power to conquer time. This we see when Clarissa again watches the old lady across the way. The question asked in a similar situation earlier in the day is now answered:

> The clock began striking. The young man had killed himself; but she did not pity him; with the clock striking the hour, one, two, three, she did not pity him, with all this going on. There! the old lady had put out her light! the whole house was dark now with this going on, she repeated, and the words came to her, Fear no more the heat of the sun. She must go back to them. But what an extraordinary night! She felt glad he had done it; thrown it away.... He made her feel the beauty; made her feel the fun. But she must go back. She must assemble. She must find Peter and Sally. And she came in from the little room (pp. 204–5).

Clarissa intuitively grasps the meaning of Septimus' vision, which he could communicate only by death. She thereby absorbs into herself the significance which Septimus holds for the reader; and yet she retains her own special power to create in the imperfect fallen realm of human relations, a power which Septimus wholly lacked. In her handling of the conclusion to this novel Mrs Woolf attempts to make clear that we must retain the limiting protecting identity which is ours in time if we are to triumph over time.

A skilful subordinate device is used throughout the book to reinforce this relationship between Septimus and Clarissa. It is the recurring tag from Shakespeare, 'Fear no more the heat of the sun,' in the passage quoted above. Early in the book Clarissa, looking into a shop window, sees a volume of Shakespeare opened at these lines, and as she reads them, she asks herself, 'What was she trying to recover? What image of white dawn in the open country?' (p. 12). Her failure to recover it suggests the inadequacy of her vague theories about the unifying power of personality, which I have already mentioned. Later on in the book Septimus, in his momentary tranquil return to the actuality of time, finds it transfigured. In the image which occurs to him, he had fallen through the sea of time into a flaming purgatorial world of terrifying and redeeming insight; now he returns to the surface to rejoice in the transfiguration of the world:

> Every power poured its treasure on his head, and his hand lay there on the back of the sofa, as he had seen his hand lie when he was bathing, floating, on the top of the waves, while far away on shore he heard dogs barking and barking far away. Fear no more, says the heart in the body; fear no more. He was not afraid. At every moment

Nature signified by some laughing hint ... Shakespeare's words, her meaning (p. 154).

For Clarissa, standing in front of the shop window, this line meant an illumination lost and not yet recovered; for Septimus it means an illumination received in its fullest intensity. When Clarissa repeats this line near the end of the book, and after Septimus' death, she recalls for the reader the groping way in which she first read it; and this stresses the fact that she now repeats it as Septimus did, with a sense of peace and reassurance. So it is that the profounder vision of Septimus is given to Clarissa without its attendant agony.

When she leaves the little room, she returns to the larger room of human relations. Our knowledge of what she has just been thinking explains the sudden strange excitement of Peter Walsh as he sees her standing in the doorway of the drawing-room: for Clarissa, returning to the party, symbolizes the transfiguration of time.

II

To the Lighthouse is the full and final expression of the synthesis first attempted in *Mrs Dalloway*. For that reason I shall limit myself to a few dogmatic remarks about the unifying and vitalizing principle of the whole book, its symbolism. Sea images, colour images, the associations of memory, recurrent verbal patterns, all serve to spin around the actual events a subtle web of interrelated meanings. The structure also is significant: the first section is called 'The Window', an image associated, as we have seen, with the individual's vision of life; the second, 'Time Passes', portrays the assault of time on the integrity of that vision; and in the third, 'The Lighthouse', the vision is triumphantly reaffirmed.

The lighthouse is the central symbol of the book, and what it means depends on who is looking at it: it has no single limited meaning, hence its power as a symbol. Its relation to Mrs Ramsay is of crucial importance, for Mrs Ramsay has the power to see what Clarissa finally saw, the transfiguration of time by eternity. But Mrs Ramsay's vision is more sophisticated. Although she sits in her room and undergoes the mystical experience of becoming the thing she looks at, the lighthouse, she nevertheless recognizes that its meaning is paradoxical: it is 'so much her, yet so little her' (p. 103); it stands firm and unchanging amid the seas of time, yet in a sense has no reality apart from the sea. Its beam revolves in a pulsing rhythm akin to that of the time process, and so, as she watches it, she calls it 'the pitiless, the remorseless' (p. 103); at the same time, however, it gives her a sense of stability, 'this peace, this rest, this eternity' (p. 100). It is not change, yet cannot be separated from change, and therefore represents a vital synthesis of time and eternity. This makes it an objective correlative for Mrs Ramsay's vision.

An objective correlative is lacking in *Mrs Dalloway*, where Clarissa, at the end, is herself the symbol of her own vision. That explains, I think, why Mrs Woolf could not follow her first intention of having Clarissa die: if she had, the meaning of Clarissa's vision would have vanished with Clarissa. It also explains why Mrs Woolf can and does let Mrs Ramsay die. It is important that she should die, for death is the most powerful assault which time can make on her vision. It sweeps her away, but it cannot destroy the lighthouse; and by the time she dies, the lighthouse has become the meaning of Mrs Ramsay.

The relationship of Mr and Mrs Ramsay repeats this idea on another level, for as husband and wife they are the lighthouse. Crudely put, Mrs Ramsay equals eternity, Mr Ramsay equals time; they are married. For Mrs Ramsay, though she triumphs in time, triumphs because she intuits eternity; and Mr Ramsay, though he loftily seeks a philosophical absolute which will solve the problem of 'subject and object and the nature of reality' (p. 40), cannot break his bondage to time without the aid of his wife. Together they fulfil each other, and are the creators of life.

In the last section the ancient mystic symbols of the Quest and the Love Union are related to the experiences of Mr Ramsay and Lily Briscoe. The completion of Lily's painting, her vision of life, involves a spiritual union with Mrs Ramsay; and Mr Ramsay's sea voyage is obviously a quest. But Lily's love union involves a quest, and Mr Ramsay's quest culminates in a love union; for as he voyages over an expanse of sea to the lighthouse, Lily voyages over an expanse of time, searching the past for the meaning of Mrs Ramsay. At the exact moment that Mrs Ramsay appears before Lily, enabling her to complete her painting, Mr Ramsay arrives at the lighthouse, and has rejoined his wife. The experiences of Lily and Mr Ramsay coincide therefore not only in time but in visionary significance as well. Both reaffirm the triumphant validity of Mrs Ramsay's vision of life.

Another set of symbols underlies this validity, performing the same function as the tag from Shakespeare in *Mrs Dalloway*. In the first section Mrs Ramsay goes to see if the children are asleep. They are not, for a boar's skull nailed on the wall has frightened Cam; and James, who loves its bare white severity, will not allow her to touch it. Mrs Ramsay drapes her green shawl over the skull, thereby creating for Cam a new world of heightened beauty and peace, at the same time assuring James that the skull is still there. In the middle section the little winds of corruption enter the abandoned house and separate shawl from skull, destroying the single visionary world created from both. In the last section Cam, staring at the rush of green waters beside her, slowly recalls that world of long ago, and feels suddenly at peace. James, gazing at the severe whiteness of the lighthouse, lonely on its bare rock, recalls how the lighthouse looked when he saw it years before with his mother, and concludes that both are true—the 'silvery, misty-looking tower' then, and the tower 'stark and straight' now (p. 311). Thus, in the children, the synthesis achieved by Mrs Ramsay is again vindicated.

If this analysis is right, then in these two novels Mrs Woolf has endeavoured to work out one of the two solutions to our original problem, for the world of mind time and the world of linear time are related to each other because both are related to a central and eternal reality.

III

The Waves is significant as a radical departure from *To the Light-house* in technique and thought. We are once again immersed in the sea of time, and its relentless pounding again opens the abyss between mind time and linear time which *To the Lighthouse* had triumphantly closed. The book is dominated by the rhythm of waves: in the poetic passages between sections, which I shall call lyrics, the sun slowly rises and falls in the sky, lending the shape of one enormous wave to the whole book; the thoughts of the characters eddy and swirl restlessly; the style surges and subsides with brilliant intensity. The dominant mood is one of anguished effort, suffering, and disillusionment: the total vision of the book is undoubtedly tragic.

While this is the major impact of *The Waves*, I wish to discuss certain other elements which redeem it from notoriety merely as a masterpiece of negation. It is my thesis that *The Waves* is an attempt to begin a new integration of the individual, not in terms of the cosmic unity found in *To the Lighthouse,* but in terms of a 'human communion'. What I mean by this phrase will, I hope, shortly appear.

When the six characters are all about twenty-five years old, they hold a farewell dinner for Percival, a seventh figure, who is leaving for India. We know Percival only through the eyes of the others, for his own consciousness is never explored; yet he is of central importance, because for the others he is a hero born to conquer the disintegrative powers of time. Like Mrs Ramsay and Clarissa, he is the unconscious doer, the artist in living, whose medium is action.

As the dinner progresses, the others feel their common love for Percival intensify until it becomes a creative act of communion with each other. Bernard, who is a novelist and the most important of the six characters, expresses clearly the significance of this communion as they leave the restaurant and he speaks of

... the swelling and splendid moment created by us from Percival. ... We have proved, sitting eating, sitting talking, that we can add to the treasury of moments. We are not slaves bound to suffer incessantly unrecorded petty blows on our bent back. We are not sheep either, following a master. We are creators. We too have made something that will join the innumerable congregations of past time. We too, as we put on our hats and push open the door, stride not into chaos, but into a world that our own force can subjugate and make part of the illumined and everlasting road (pp. 104-5).

Now the 'moment' here is very different from what it was in *Mrs Dalloway* and *To the Lighthouse*: it no longer comes involuntarily or as a result of passive receptivity, it must be created; and it no longer consists in an intuition of a mystical cosmic reality unifying the worlds of mind and linear time. The world of the time-process 'out there' is now something which man must subjugate: he is a creator. This ardent sense of their own power is evoked by their communion, in which they lose the selfhoods imposed on them by time and become, in the image used, 'a whole flower, to which every eye brings its own contribution' (p. 91). Now the experience of creating this single identity lasts only a moment; but the communion created in that moment is eternal. It joins the 'innumerable congregations of past time' in a celebration of the larger body of Man, which exists in an everlasting Now.

It is significant that Percival is about to leave for India, a wasteland waiting to be rescued, where the luxuriant powers of nature reign triumphantly over impotent humanity. And it is significant that as he leaves he is bade by Bernard to look at the lights of the city blending in 'the yellow canopy of our tremendous energy' (p. 105), the material expression of the promethean powers of man. Percival, the protagonist of these powers, the god of action, is at the height of his glory; for in the lyric which follows his departure the sun is described as being at its zenith.

Once at its zenith, however, the sun must decline: Percival is thrown from his horse in India and is killed. Now time begins its subtle warfare of attrition against the meaning of Percival. The others forget him and go their separate ways: the 'tremendous energy' which he symbolized wanes within them, and in the world of action they feel that they have failed. Their lives have hardened into fixed patterns of behaviour, and they have lost any clear pattern of understanding. Then, when they are middle-aged, Bernard calls them together for a reunion dinner.

At this dinner the same communion is created, reaching its culmination as the six friends leave the restaurant and walk arm-in-arm into a park:

> 'The flower,' said Bernard, 'the red carnation that stood in the vase on the table of the restaurant when we dined together with Percival, has become a six-sided flower; made of six lives.'
>
> 'A mysterious illumination,' said Louis, 'visible against those yew trees.'
>
> 'Built up with much pain, many strokes,' said Jinny.

'Marriage, death, travel, friendship,' said Bernard; 'town and country; children and all that; a many-sided substance cut out of this dark; a many-faceted flower. Let us stop for a moment; let us behold what we have made. Let it blaze against those yew trees. One life. There. It is over. Gone out.' (p. 162).

This needs little comment, in the light of the first dinner, but we might note that this single life is *cut from* the darkness of time, and burns *against* that darkness and *against* the yew trees of death.

At this dinner, however, Percival is absent; and the special promise which he symbolized has not been fulfilled. What was then the future has become the past, and as they lived it they did not conquer it. Now it is too late for action: as the sun declines it is time to seek understanding. That is why Bernard, the novelist, who seeks understanding before all things, dominates the dinner.

The new stature of Bernard is made clear in the last section of the book, where he sums up the meaning of his life. In it three notes are sounded. The first is that of constant warfare against the enemy, time. The second is the rejection of the idea that an eternal reality 'out there' underlies and unifies the time-process. As a youth, Bernard recalls, he believed that the willow tree pointed to something 'beyond and outside our own predicament; to that which is symbolic, and thus perhaps permanent'; now he dismisses the willow tree as one of those 'phantoms made of dust . . . mutable, vain' (pp. 176, 202). There is no trace of the vision of Septimus Smith, for whom Nature's meaning was, 'Fear no more the heat of the sun'; and there is no lighthouse to guide us over the waves. Against his progressive disillusionment stands only the saving reality of the human communion enjoyed at the two dinner-parties, and this is the third emphasis in his summing-up. He recalls the reunion dinner, and how 'we saw for a moment laid out among us the body of the complete human being whom we have failed to be, but at the same time, cannot forget' (p. 196). As the dinner progressed, however, their temporal identities fell away, this body rose, and they became it: 'I saw blaze bright Neville, Jinny, Rhoda, Louis, Susan, and myself, our life, our identity . . . we six, out of many million millions, for one moment out of what measureless abundance of past time and time to come, burnt there triumphant. The moment was all; the moment was enough' (p. 197). With a special awareness of their communion he leaves the restaurant in which he has been sitting and stands outside, watching the dawn rise, and facing the antagonist in the final passage of the book:

I am aware once more of a new desire, something rising beneath me like the proud horse whose rider first spurs and then pulls him back. What enemy do we now perceive advancing against us, you whom I ride now, as we stand pawing this stretch of pavement? It is death. Death is the enemy. It is death against whom I ride with

my spear couched and my hair flying back like a young man's, like
Percival's, when he galloped in India. I strike spurs into my horse.
Against you I will fling myself, unvanquished and unyielding, O
Death!

> *The waves broke on the shore* (p. 211).

Bernard dies. (That is the meaning of the final sentence, which is
italicized, and so belongs with the lyrics, not with Bernard's final
thoughts.) As an individual he breaks on the shore. But he is much
more than an individual: throughout his summing-up, he slowly sheds
his private selfhood and absorbs into himself the identities of the other
six. This is indicated, for example, by the way in which he applies to
himself images which, throughout the book, have been associated only
with the others. They are types of humanity, and Bernard thus
becomes the archetype of the race as it struggles with its creative powers
against the tyranny of time. That is why Bernard, the archetype of
vision, finally absorbs into himself the special significance of Percival,
the archetype of action; for on both levels we must ride against the
enemy. The visionary struggle is stressed, however, since Percival rises
again only through the effort of Bernard. It is significant that the
situation here is the reverse of what it was in *Mrs Dalloway*, where
Clarissa, the artist in living, absorbed into herself the meaning of
Septimus, the visionary.

Bernard thus assumes the proportions of the dragon-killer, the god
who subdues chaos: he rides with 'spear couched' like some St George.
He rides for the creation of the complete human being whom they
have failed to be yet cannot forget, a spiritual being existing on a level
untouchable by time. It is no accident that while the lyric at the
beginning of the summing-up described the disappearance of the sun
in darkness, Bernard at the end sees the dawn whitening the sky. While
as an individual he sinks into death, he also rises as the champion of
the complete human being, and becomes that being, like a dying-and-
rising god.

I repeat that these remarks concern the effort which Mrs Woolf is
making to achieve a new integration of the individual. That effort is
not successful in *The Waves*, which is primarily the tragedy of the
individual wave breaking on the shore. Nevertheless, we find here
the initial formulation of a synthesis which receives consummate
expression in *Between the Acts*.

IV

The main structural device of *Between the Acts* is simple and
venerable, that of a play within a play. There is the pageant staged in
the garden, which I shall call the microcosmic pageant; and there is
the macrocosmic pageant which goes on before and after the small

pageant, and between its acts. My chief interest is in the relationship between these two pageants. The proscenium arch for both of them is a carefully fostered sense of our community in time, which frames and illuminates the present moment unfolding on the stage. All through the book a host of details sustains our feeling that the past is present.

The macrocosmic pageant unfolds for the first hundred pages and centres on the interplay of tensions between the main characters of the book. On a sleepy afternoon these tensions increase until, by the time the pageant is staged, each character is isolated from the rest. Bart Oliver, a disciple of reason, is at odds with his sister, Lucy Swithin, a disciple of faith who is addicted to an imaginative reconstruction of the past. Giles Oliver and his wife Isa embody the impulses to creative action and creative vision which we have noted in previous novels. Both are frustrated by the sequence of events. Giles, a man of action, is oppressed by time past (his life as a respectable stockbroker) and by time future (the impending war in Europe, which he can oppose with no constructive or even destructive action). His intense frustration leads him into childish infidelities to his wife, who partly symbolizes for him the oppressive sequence of events. Ironically, he stands in part for the same thing in her eyes; but she longs to escape from the burden of time into an inner world of absolute knowledge and beauty, not into a world of liberating action, and so writes poetry about her longing to 'lose what binds us here' (p. 21). They both love and hate each other; the tension between them is not resolved until the last page of the book, and even then only by implication.

The brooding and vague antagonism which settles over them all is partly broken and partly aggravated by Mrs Manresa, a 'wild child of nature' (p. 52), who surrenders eagerly to the flux of time, seeking no other absolute.

The actors and audience now arrive and the microcosmic pageant begins. There are four acts in it, and I shall consider the first three in a general way only, in order to concentrate on the last. At the start of the pageant, and through most of the acts, a chorus of villagers winds its way among the trees which form the backdrop, chanting words half-audible to the audience; for the winds of time blow away the meaning of the anonymous millions of the past. The words we do hear emphasize the tenacious endurance of the race in time; whatever period of history is passing on the stage, the chorus is always the same.

The first act is an Elizabethan tragedy. Its details need not concern us, for along with all the other acts its value lies in the reactions of the audience to it. As Isa watches it she realizes that the plot, a special pattern in past time, is unimportant, and that the meaning of the play is the timeless glory and terror of love, hate, and death. But immediately after the death of one of the characters in it, the actors come forward and join in a dance. As they whirl about, laughing and shouting, the audience too begins to laugh, to clap, to join in spirit this dance of irrepressible life. It is then, as the author of the pageant, Miss La Trobe, intended, that the members of the audience *become* the Elizabethans.

After the dance an interval occurs in which tea is served in the barn. Now the macrocosmic drama is resumed. The actors do not realize that they are acting it, and for this reason the connections between the two pageants must be implied. I have space to illustrate this technique only by one example. As Lucy Swithin sits in the barn, she watches the swallows flying among the rafters and thinks how they came to this spot 'before there was a channel, when the earth, upon which this Windsor chair was planted, was a riot of rhododendrons'. At this point Mrs Manresa bustles up.

> 'I was hoping you'd tell me,' said Mrs Manresa. 'Was it an old play? Was it a new play?'
> No one answered.
> 'Look!' Lucy exclaimed.
> 'The birds?' said Mrs Manresa, looking up (p. 130).

The birds are the answer to her question. The play is as old as the swallows coming ages ago; and as new as the swallows swooping above them in the present moment.

The next act is cut on the pattern of Restoration comedy, and ironically modifies the grand themes of hate and love and death presented in the previous act. Now we see vanity, deceit, lust, greed, the absurdity and pathos of old age, the power and cruelty of youth. One is struck by the vigour and humour of the satire; Mrs Woolf's hypersensitivity to the depravity of human beings is by this time less agonized and more robust. For Septimus Smith, the only terror he could not face was the depravity of men, and so he turned towards the centre. Now, however, *we* are the centre, and must face ourselves unflinchingly. Our depravity cannot be explained away; but in our attitude to it lies the measure of its power, which will be reduced to a minimum if met without illusion and with purifying laughter. No one in the book flees, as Septimus fled, to seek in death eternal life.

Yet we have eternal life, and its nature is suggested by Mrs Swithin between the acts, when she seeks out Miss La Trobe:

> She gazed at Miss La Trobe with a cloudless old-aged stare. Their eyes met in a common effort to bring a common meaning to birth. They failed; and Mrs Swithin, laying hold desperately of a fraction of her meaning, said: 'What a small part I've had to play! But you've made me feel I could have played ... Cleopatra!'
> 'I might have been—Cleopatra,' Miss La Trobe repeated. 'You've stirred in me my unacted part,' she meant. . . .
> 'You've twitched the invisible strings,' was what the old lady meant; and revealed—of all people—Cleopatra! Glory possessed

her. Ah, but she was not merely a twitcher of individual strings; she was one who seethes wandering bodies and floating voices in a cauldron, and makes rise up from the amorphous mass a recreated world (pp. 179–80).

Miss La Trobe, the artist in vision, arouses in Lucy the slumbering power of imaginative vision which enables Lucy to see that on a level of being of which she is rarely conscious she lives at all times.

In the next act of the pageant the Victorians are exuberantly parodied. The two pageants are now merging in historical focus, since many among the audience have themselves lived during the age of faith in fossils and fossil faiths, now so ruthlessly mocked. But Mrs Swithin makes the truly significant comment when Isa asks incredulously if the Victorians were really like that:

'The Victorians,' Mrs Swithin mused. 'I don't believe,' she said with her odd little smile, 'that there ever were such people. Only you and me and William dressed differently.'
'You don't believe in history,' said William (p. 203).

Neither does Mrs Woolf. This pageant about history is a declaration that history itself is not leading us anywhere in particular. Yet we cannot escape it. Immediately after this act, a cloud-burst briefly showers the audience. Isa, for whom history is a burden to be lost in the attainment of some absolute, looks up: ' "O that our human pain could here have ending!" Isa murmured. Looking up she received two great blots of rain full on her face. They trickled down her cheeks as if they were her own tears. But they were all people's tears, weeping for all people' (p. 210). This is the darker aspect of our communion, the community in bondage which we share under the tyranny of time.

With sorrow still gripping them the audience watches a tableau; a man and a woman are shown rebuilding a ruined wall. This is the task which confronts them as the inheritors in time of a civilization fallen into disrepair. As the audience watches in silence, all of the actors who have taken part in the pageant dance out onto the stage, each declaiming some lines from his particular role in history, and carrying a mirror or some shiny object which will reflect the members of the audience to themselves. At this effrontery only Mrs Manresa retains her poise: she seizes the opportunity to lean forward and powder her nose. This is only natural, since she has no other identity besides that reflected in the mirror of the present moment. The rest feel they have, however, and resent the necessity of facing their time-bound selves. Some of them are only restrained from leaving by a 'megaphonic, anonymous, loudspeaking' voice from the bushes.

The voice sums up both the satirical and constructive visions of Miss La Trobe, demanding first that the audience cast away illusions, and concluding with the bitter exhortation, '*Look at ourselves, ladies*

and gentlemen! Then at the wall; and ask how's this wall ... civiliza-
tion, to be built by (here the mirrors flicked and flashed) *orts, scraps*
and fragments like ourselves?' (p. 219).

Then the voice turns to another theme—our greatness, reflected,
for example, in ' *"the resolute refusal of some pimpled dirty little*
scrub in sandals to sell his soul. There is such a thing—you can't
deny it. What? You can't descry it? All you can see of yourself is
scraps, orts and fragments? Well then listen to the gramophone affirm-
ing." ' Here is what the gramophone affirms:

> Like quicksilver sliding, filings magnetized, the distracted united.
> The tune began; the first note meant a second; the second a third.
> Then down beneath a force was born in opposition; then another. On
> different levels they diverged. On different levels ourselves went
> forward; flower gathering some on the surface; others descending to
> wrestle with the meaning; but all comprehending; all enlisted. The
> whole population of the mind's immeasurable profundity came
> flocking; ... from chaos and cacophony measure; but not the melody
> of surface sound alone controlled it; but also the warring battle-
> plumed warriors straining asunder: To part? No. Compelled from
> the ends of the horizon; recalled from the edge of appalling
> crevasses; they crashed; solved; united. ...
>
> Was that voice ourselves? Scraps, orts and fragments, are we,
> also, that? (pp. 220–1).

We all comprehend and enlist in the creation of a total harmony,
the imaginative totality of our human life. This is the meaning of the
music; and of Miss La Trobe's pageant; and of Mrs Woolf's book.
This theme is emphasized later on when the Rev. G. W. Streatfield
prosily remarks that ' "To me at least it was indicated that we are
members one of another. Each is part of the whole ... We act different
parts; but are the same" ' (pp. 223–6). Or again, as the crowd leaves,
amid idle chatter flash remarks luminous with the significance of all
that has gone before. One of these is put in a question: 'The looking-
glasses now—did they mean the reflection is the dream; and the music
... is the truth?' (p. 234). The reflections in the glass are only our
temporal identities; but the communion expressed in the music is
our eternal identity.

After the crowd has gone we return to the macrocosmic pageant.
But the characters in it are now enlarged: behind them is the meaning
of the small pageant, and they are now acting in two plays. When Mrs
Manresa walks towards her car 'like a goddess, buoyant, abundant,
with flower-chained captives following in her wake', she is more than
Mrs Manresa—she is one whole aspect of our life. So are the others
as they linger in the dusk.

Miss La Trobe, the artist, prepares to leave, now that the audience
is gone and she need not face them. Looking back on her pageant she

sees that in the effort to communicate her vision lay glory; and that in her partial failure to do so lies the inevitable bondage of the artist to his own limitations, to his audience, and to his medium. Nevertheless, she cannot abandon the effort. As she leaves Pointz Hall another play begins to stir in her mind. ' "I should group them," she murmured, "here." It would be midnight; there would be two figures, half-concealed by a rock. The curtain would rise. What would the first words be? The words escaped her' (p. 246). Later, however, as she sits in a pub she again visualizes the scene: 'There was the high ground at midnight; there the rock; and two scarcely perceptible figures. . . . She set down her glass. She heard the first words.'

Now as Miss La Trobe sits in the pub, the actors in the macrocosmic drama at Pointz Hall sit quietly in the drawing-room, reading the paper and looking over the day's mail. For the reader, however, they are playing two dramas at once. Slowly the light fades, the sky becomes cold and severe. Bart rises and stalks silently from the room. Lucy closes her outline of history and tiptoes out. Now Giles and Isa are alone: they rise.

> Left alone for the first time that day they were silent. Alone, enmity was bared; also love. Before they slept, they must fight; after they had fought they would embrace. From that embrace another life might be born. But first they must fight, as the dog fox fights with the vixen, in the heart of darkness, in the fields of night.
>
> Isa let her sewing drop. The great hooded chairs had become enormous. And Giles too. And Isa too against the window. The window was all sky without colour. The house had lost its shelter. It was night before roads were made, or houses. It was the night that dwellers in caves had watched from some high place among rocks.
>
> Then the curtain rose. They spoke (pp. 255–6).

These are the concluding words of the book. They verify the vision of Miss La Trobe: for this is the scene which she visualizes in the pub; and the words she hears are the words which are about to be spoken as the curtain rises and the book ends. In this way the pageant which she staged earlier in the day, like this new pageant she is creating, is revealed as not merely a reconstruction of the past but as a prophetic insight into the essential reality of human life at all times and places.

This effect is reinforced at the end because the reader suddenly is related to the novel in the same way that Giles and Isa are related to Miss La Trobe's pageant. Throughout the book Giles and Isa have watched a pageant which they consider an interpretation of their life; suddenly, at the end, the reader sees that it *is* their life. Then he feels in full the impact of the novel as an interpretation of *his* life, because the novel as a whole is a pageant occurring literally *between the acts* of the drama which the reader himself plays before and after reading it. The effect of this device is to intensify and to expand the vision of the book. Its scope suddenly widens from the limits of the events in it to include the events of the reader's own experience. When the curtain rises at the end, he closes the book and carries on the ensuing drama himself.

The vision of this book is clearly tragic. Shrouded in the sheltering and obscuring medium of time, Giles and Isa loom immense and representative, Man and Woman, gripped by the primeval necessities of love and hate and creation. From the complex interaction of these forces and others rises our eternal life; this is the deepest significance of Miss La Trobe's vision. The tragedy is that Giles and Isa, ourselves, do not retain their vision of this redeeming reality. They see in a glass darkly, a fact which leads Miss La Trobe to include comedy and tragedy in her pageant. But the comedy of our situation is so profound that it is almost indistinguishable from tragedy. Isa and Giles struggle and cleave together in 'the heart of darkness, the fields of night'. In the darkness their grandeur is titanic, but it is the grandeur of beings doomed to ceaseless struggle against the power on which they depend for existence.

There is no exultantly triumphant vision in *Between the Acts;* but it is a moot point whether a tragic vision of life can be called, as many have called this book, utterly negative. Although the luminous evasions of *To the Lighthouse* have been abandoned, the essential affirmation of the value of life remains, disenchanted but not destroyed.

Of the two solutions to our original problem it embodies the second —that is, the effort to find in one of the two worlds of mind and linear time an absolute. For *Between the Acts* means nothing less than this: if we would be saved, we must, through the exercise of our creative powers of mind and imagination, recreate time in our own image.

From 'Time in the Novels of Virginia Woolf', *University of Toronto Quarterly,* Vol. 18, 1949, pp. 186–201. Since publication the author's views have undergone some change, and he would now qualify the rather schematic conclusions reached above.

JAMES HAFLEY

Symbolism in *The Voyage Out*

... Nearly every action, nearly every event in *The Voyage Out* is
made to be symbolical. Thus there are two voyages: the voyage *out*
from London to South America, and the voyage *in* from Santa Marina
to a native camp on the bank of the Amazon. The first of these
voyages, occupying the first six chapters of the novel, serves at once
to set the stage and to suggest Rachel's voyage to an understanding of
life and experience; the second, occurring shortly after the climax of
the novel—shortly after Rachel and Terence fall in love—coincides
with Rachel's voyage to an understanding of herself. The tragedy here
is at once Rachel's death and her inability to unite her own world
with the world around her. When she has come to an understanding
of the world around her, Rachel first becomes puzzled about herself
as an individual in this world. It is this dispute between the individual
and society with which the novel is primarily concerned. Thus the
Villa San Gervasio, where Rachel lives with Helen and Ridley
Ambrose, represents the individual's world, and the hotel below it
represents the social world.

In Chapter 8 Helen and Rachel go for a walk from the villa down
to the hotel, where they have not been before. Walking around the
outside terrace, they look into one window after another: dining room,
kitchen, drawing room, lounge. Inside the lounge, the hotel's largest
room, are Terence Hewet and his brilliant friend St John Hirst; Hirst
catches sight of the two onlookers, and the women flee. The reader,
however, remains. In Chapter 9 the tour of rooms is continued: each
bedroom holds its individual, but this unity is part of the diversity
of the whole. The diversity itself, however, resolves into the unity of
the hotel—as a structural unit, the social world is very similar to the
individual world of the villa. Later Rachel goes on a personal tour of
individual bedrooms in the hotel: she has grasped the world around
her as a unit with various facets but must now come to grips with its
diversity. She has seen the inhabitants of the hotel in the lounge, at a
dance during which she herself plays the music for the dancers; now
she begins to answer invitations to 'Come and see my room'. She
must recognize the unit of people in terms of each member's
individuality. This problem of communication appears in various ways
throughout the novel.

When Rachel leaves the hotel and goes out into the sunlight, she
finds a group of people united around a tea table. One of this group,

Mrs Flushing, invites Rachel to come for a trip along the Amazon, and Rachel accepts—thus beginning the catastrophe of the novel.

This second voyage, then—the voyage *in*—symbolizes Rachel's discovery of herself and her retirement into herself. Just as the first voyage is compared to the voyages of Spanish and Elizabethan English adventurers—and Rachel's discovery compared to theirs—so this second voyage is compared to that of an explorer named Mackenzie, who 'had died of fever some ten years ago, almost within reach of civilization . . . the man who went farther inland than anyone's been yet.'[1] Again, 'they seemed to be driving into the heart of the night, for the trees closed in front of them. . . . The great darkness had the usual effect of taking away all desire for communication by making their words sound thin and small.' Each incident of this journey has its symbolic value in terms of the theme. The journey reaches its climax in a love scene between Rachel and Terence, after which both are silent and blissfully content in a story-book peace and unity. Rachel, indeed, does not even see Mackenzie's hut when it is pointed out to them and his story told. She is completely absorbed in herself and in Terence. Love, marriage—these are the words she savours as the journey continues inland and the heat becomes more and more oppressive. 'This is happiness,' she says. Rachel's is the typical tragic situation: the very thing that is to redeem her—her love for Terence—is also to cause her death. Love has not only helped Rachel to discover herself, but has also led her to reject all outside herself. To see oneself as reality and the social world as illusion, then, is fatal.

Terence—who is able to adapt his own world to the world outside himself—returns from the journey; Rachel remains in the jungle of her world and denies the world outside. Finally, however, Rachel must lose even Terence, for despite their love he cannot enter into her individual world. In the delirium that results from her sickness Rachel does not know Terence; just before her death she smiles and speaks to him, but it is then too late.

The rift between Terence and Rachel begins when they argue about whether or not they are to go to the hotel. Terence, of course, wishes to have tea with Mrs Thornbury in return for her kindnesses: he wishes to bring his relationship with Rachel to the social world. 'He wanted other people; he wanted Rachel to see him with them.' Finally Rachel yields, goes to the hotel, endures the congratulations. In the afternoon she starts to have a severe headache; her final illness has begun.

Rachel is the central character of *The Voyage Out*, but Terence Hewet's behaviour—not Rachel's—is in accord with the perspective. This novel would be pathos rather than tragedy if Rachel's death were offered as the normal solution to the problem it presents. The last chapter makes clear the fact that Rachel's attitude is wrong and

---

[1] Cf. Conrad's *Heart of Darkness*, where the pattern is very similar.

Terence's right. St John Hirst, who has been Rachel Vinrace's counterpart throughout the novel, is the key figure in the last pages. He comes back from the villa to the hotel, over which Rachel's death has cast an unnatural sobriety of mood. It is night when he arrives at the hotel, and a storm—which comes to symbolize the 'life itself' against which both individual and social life are placed—contrasts with the hotel's guests gathered together in the lounge. Gradually, despite their sorrow for Rachel, these people have resumed their normal occupations: they are knitting, reading, talking, playing chess. Hirst, who has walked from the villa through the storm, feels suddenly quite secure when he looks at them in the warm, comfortable room. He is turning from Rachel's position to Terence's. The lightning flashes, and spreads 'a broad illumination over the earth'. Conversation goes on, the chess game concludes. 'All these voices sounded gratefully in St John's ears as he lay half-asleep, and yet vividly conscious of everything around him. Across his eyes passed a procession of objects, black and indistinct, the figures of people picking up their books, their cards, their balls of wool, their work-baskets, and passing him one after another on their way to bed.' Neither the individual world nor the social world is complete within itself; the two must blend together. Both are finite, but 'life itself' is one and infinite. Of this last there is only a suggestion in Virginia Woolf's first novel; the problem of 'life itself' will be explored later. . . .

From Chapter 2 of *The Glass Roof: Virginia Woolf as a Novelist*, University of California Press, Berkeley, 1954, pp. 15–19.

A. D. MOODY

Mrs *Dalloway* as Comedy

... Perhaps it should be stated quite clearly that Clarissa Dalloway is not, as many critics have taken her to be, a character whom Virginia Woolf simply admires and endorses. The treatment of her, as of her society, is consistently critical; and though her surface brilliance and vivacity evoke a sympathetic response in the writing, there is also a steady judgment of her deep inadequacy, a grave insistence upon the dissipation and death of her spirit in glittering triviality.

However, the novel is rather a portrait of Mrs Dalloway's society than of the lady herself. The 'material' of which it is made is the life, in London following the Great War, of a small segment of English society—'the British ruling class' as it is called in the book. And this life is brought into focus in the character of 'Clarissa Dalloway'. The way in which she is characteristic, and what it is she characterizes, can be shown from the opening section, in which she walks from her house in Westminster to buy flowers in Bond Street. It becomes clear that her life is not much more than vivacity, and that the world she loves and builds round herself is a tissue of shallow impressions and fantasies. The 'divine vitality', which she declares she adores, is manifested in cabs passing, sandwich men shuffling and swinging, brass bands and barrel organs; that is, in the mere sensations of noise and movement and excitement. Moreover, there is so little difference between this 'life' and her equally superficial notions of death, that the terms in which she expresses this latter apply just as well to the former—as the ambiguous present tense brings out in this passage:

> what she loved was this, here, now, in front of her; the fat lady in the cab. Did it matter then, she asked herself, walking towards Bond Street, did it matter that she must inevitably cease completely; all this must go on without her; did she resent it; or did it not become consoling to believe that death ended absolutely? but that somehow in the streets of London, on the ebb and flow of things, here, there, she survived, Peter survived, lived in each other.... (p. 11).

This reinforces the impression that Clarissa Dalloway's actual life, so much a matter of existing in the ebb and flow of things, is virtually a non-life. She is shown to be of not much interest in herself; she has to offer only a sharp awareness of the surface of her world and its people. This makes her something of an animated mirror, having a life made up of the world she reflects. But to be and to do that is precisely her function for the novel: she is a living image of the surface of the society Virginia Woolf was concerned with.

At the same time she is a criticism of her society. For the proposition that she is what she reflects holds true as well in its converse form: that is, her society is what it is seen to be in her; and her character, such as it is, is the character of her society. If her life is a kind of non-life, so too is the life of her society as a whole. So, in this passage, the quality of its way of life is precisely evoked, and evaluated, in Clarissa Dalloway's stiltedly conventional fantasy:

> The War was over, except for someone like Mrs Foxcroft at the Embassy last night eating her heart out because that nice boy was killed and now the old Manor House must go to a cousin; or Lady Bexborough who opened a bazaar, they said, with the telegram in her hand, John, her favourite, killed; but it was over; thank Heaven— over. It was June. The King and Queen were at the Palace. And everywhere, though it was still so early, there was a beating, a stirring of galloping ponies, tapping of cricket bats; Lords, Ascot, Ranelagh and all the rest of it; wrapped in the soft mesh of the grey-blue morning air, which, as the day wore on, would unwind them, and set down on their lawns and pitches the bouncing ponies, whose forefeet just struck the ground and up they sprung, the whirling young men, and laughing girls in their transparent muslins, who, even now, after dancing all night, were taking their absurd woolly dogs for a run.... (pp. 6–7).

There Clarissa Dalloway and her society merge the one into the other. The style is an index at once to her sensibility, and to the quality of the life of her world. And in both there is the same governing impulse to turn away from the disturbing depths of feeling, and towards a conventional pleasantness or sentimentality or frivolousness. In short, the life of Clarissa Dalloway's society as a whole is here characterized by that deadness of spirit which makes her what she is.

Clarissa Dalloway is then something more than an image of 'the British ruling class'. She comes to embody as well Virginia Woolf's criticism of the life of that class, to be, therefore, the focus of the criticism which is the main concern of the novel.

It may be possible to give at least a bare indication of how this criticism is worked out, and what it amounts to in the work as a whole, by examining a crucial paragraph. This is the moment of fulfilment at the climax of her party to which Clarissa Dalloway's day, and indeed her whole life, has been directed:

> Indeed, Clarissa felt, the Prime Minister had been good to come. And, walking down the room with him, with Sally there and Peter there and Richard very pleased, with all those people rather inclined, perhaps, to envy, she had felt that intoxication of the

D

moment, that dilation of the nerves of the heart itself till it seemed to quiver, steeped, upright;—yes, but after all it was what other people felt, that; for, though she loved it and felt it tingle and sting, still these semblances, these triumphs (dear old Peter, for example, thinking her so brilliant), had a hollowness; at arm's length they were, not in the heart.... (pp. 191–2).

Virtually the whole of Clarissa Dalloway's life and society is involved here by implication. The movement of feeling is the mere matter of a moment; but it gathers to itself a reverberant context of associated ironies; and these question and evaluate the moment of triumph, and, in doing so, bring into a critical order the varieties of experience with which the novel has been concerned. This order is based, just here, in the two main images, that of the Prime Minister, and that of the heart which is hollow. There is as well a good deal of detail working in a subsidiary way to enrich the general effect. Clarissa's word 'upright', for example, has been probed in earlier contexts, so that here it carries associations which ironically question its affirmative tone. But it will be enough here to consider only the main effects.

First there are the associations accumulated about the image of the Prime Minister, which amount, in sum, to a considerable comic sketch. Peter Walsh had direly warned Clarissa that 'She would marry a Prime Minister and stand at the top of a staircase; the perfect hostess.' But that was very nearly her ambition. Seeing a closed car in Bond Street, which might contain the Prime Minister, if it is not the Queen or the Prince of Wales, she imagines him disappearing

> to blaze among candelabras, glittering stars, breasts stiff with oak leaves, Hugh Whitbread and all his colleagues, the gentlemen of England, that night in Buckingham Palace. And Clarissa, too, gave a party. She stiffened a little; so she would stand at the top of her stairs (p. 20).

This, the prelude to the comedy, is developed in an immediately following passage to involve her social world at large:

> Gliding across Piccadilly, the car turned down St James's Street. Tall men, men of robust physique, well-dressed men with their tail-coats and their white slips and their hair raked back, who, for reasons difficult to discriminate, were standing in the bow window of White's with their hands behind the tails of their coats, looking out, perceived instinctively that greatness was passing, and the pale light of the immortal presence fell upon them as it had fallen upon Clarissa Dalloway. At once they stood even straighter, and removed their hands, and seemed ready to attend their Sovereign, if need be, to the cannon's mouth, as their ancestors had done before them.... (p. 21).

This passage of caricature quite devastatingly defines the attitudes by which Clarissa Dalloway measures her social triumph. It comes near the beginning of the book, it is true: but it is kept dramatically alive throughout the whole, particularly in the satiric observation of Hugh Whitbread. And it is picked up explicitly, just before Clarissa's supreme moment, when the Prime Minister appears in person at her party. Peter Walsh sees that he looks a nonentity: 'You might have stood him behind a counter and bought biscuits—poor chap, all rigged up in gold lace'; and it is immediately clear that it is the mere symbol, the gold lace, that matters: 'it was perfectly plain that they all knew, felt to the marrow of their bones, this majesty passing; this symbol of what they all stood for, English society' (p. 189). The very considerable comedy developed about that symbol provides the measure, at once, of the extent to which Clarissa Dalloway's sense of triumph is representative of the values of her society, and of their intrinsic worth. Her triumph is, unmistakably, the triumph of empty honour.

But the comedy does not serve merely to 'place' her emotion. For her emotion is part of the comedy; and indeed her triumph is its denouement, the moment in which the play of social honour and spiritual emptiness is resolved into a more profound perception. In itself her reaction into a recognition of the sterility of what she has valued—'at arm's length they were, not in the heart'—simply endorses the valuation which has been felt in the writing throughout. Its importance is that it touches for the first time directly upon the reality beneath the social veneer, and, with that, effects a shift from the mode of light comedy into something more serious:

> and suddenly, as she saw the Prime Minister go down the stairs, the gilt rim of the Sir Joshua picture of the little girl with a muff brought back Kilman with a rush; Kilman her enemy. That was satisfying; that was real. Ah, how she hated her—... (p. 192).

Her hatred of Miss Kilman shows her state to be worse than mere superficiality: her cultivated surface has masked something evil. For, as her reaction here reveals, when the life of feeling and inward understanding is denied, it does not simply wither away, but becomes the enemy of life; the soul that is dead and yet in life, lives to be the agent of death.

Her revelation of herself in that moment relates her unmistakably to Sir William Bradshaw, who is certainly evil in the sense defined before. This is a structural connection of central importance. The comedy developed about the Prime Minister established the surface valuations of Clarissa Dalloway's triumph; but upon this connection depends the penetration of the novel in depth. . . .

From Chapter 2 of *Virginia Woolf*, Oliver and Boyd, Edinburgh and London, 1963, pp. 19-25.

Clarissa Dalloway's 'Double'

... In her preface to *Mrs Dalloway,* Virginia Woolf is explicit about the relation of Septimus Warren Smith—whose last hours form the novel's sub-plot—to the heroine. He 'is intended to be her double'. Taking [Conrad's] *The Secret Sharer* as the paradigm, we can expect Septimus' qualities to be indications, by contrast, of a lack or dark place in Mrs Dalloway, much as Leggatt illuminated the dim regions of the captain's psyche. Virginia Woolf's handling of her theme is more intricate and many-faceted than Conrad's profound but simple fable, and so the correlation between self and 'double' is not so clear-cut. The two elements essential to the myth, however, are present: a leading character who is incomplete, and the catalytic double.

We are told several times—by Clarissa herself and by Peter—that there is some emptiness in her. Peter, on his first visit to her in years, thinks: 'Shall I tell her ... or not? He would like to make a clean breast of it all. But she is too cold.' He speaks again later, of 'this coldness, this woodenness, something very profound in her'. Clarissa's own feeling about the want in her nature is connected with her husband.

> Suddenly there came a moment—for example on the river beneath the woods at Cliveden—when, through some contraction of this cold spirit, she had failed him. And then at Constantinople, and again and again. She could see what she lacked. ... It was something central which permeated; something warm which broke up surfaces and rippled the cold contact of man and woman, or of women together. For *that* one could dimly perceive.

Clarissa's position here can be compared to that of the captain at the opening of *The Secret Sharer.* Both characters recognize their lack of completeness, but its nature is as yet 'dimly perceived'; and both are (at this moment, and alone) powerless to see more clearly. At any rate, we are assured, by both Peter and Clarissa, that the shadow in her is 'something central', 'very profound'; and it assumes an even greater depth when Peter wakes suddenly, thinking of her, with the phrase, 'the death of the soul', on his lips.

> It was her manner that annoyed him; timid; hard; something arrogant; unimaginative; prudish; 'the death of the soul'. He had said that instinctively, ticketing the moment as he used to do—the death of her soul.

Even when allowances have been made for dramatic necessity in the drawing of Peter's own failures of sensibility, and his overstatement of the case, this passage must be taken as serious and crucial. The coldness at the centre of Mrs Dalloway is something mortally dangerous, threatening the icy death of the spirit. One is reminded of a couplet by Auden—

> And the seas of pity lie
> Locked and frozen in each eye.

Clarissa's progress toward selfhood is at the same time an unlocking and unfreezing of the chill at the depths, releasing in her the seas of pity. This idea is suggested by a further transmutation of the water imagery used by Virginia Woolf. 'It was ... something warm which broke up surfaces and rippled the cold contact' of one human being with another. The breaking of surfaces brings one into contact not only with the sources of one's own nature, but simultaneously with the similar sources in every human nature. Knowledge of self is achieved by, and leads to, sympathetic identity with others.

Turning from the heroine to her counterpart, we find in Septimus, first of all and most obviously, the irrationality that can be detected in Conrad's Leggatt. The original secret sharer emerges from a symbolic unconscious—the ocean; Septimus is mad, and he too has visited the sleeping depths: 'I leant over the edge of the boat and fell down, he thought. I went under the sea. I have been dead, and yet am now alive.' In them both, some of the hidden impulses at the roots of our nature are exposed. One of Virginia Woolf's early notes on *Mrs Dalloway* records her intention to present 'the world seen by the sane and the insane side by side—something like that'.[1] As it turned out, the relationship was not only parallel, but complementary. Septimus is the self standing behind Clarissa's image as she gazes into the mirror. In *The Secret Sharer*, the secret self merges with the mirrored self, but the *rapport* between Clarissa and her double must be achieved without a physical confrontation. Septimus' reality for her is on the plane of imagination. Reflected in him, nevertheless, is the failure of feeling that can be observed in Clarissa herself. After the war, 'something failed him; he could not feel'. The real truth is, of course, that Septimus has felt too deeply, has been shaken and numbed by shell shock and the war, specifically by the death of his friend Evans; his feeling has flowed through channels deeper than any so far sounded by Clarissa. But he has never gone beyond the first paralyzing numbness to see, consciously, the reality of his emotion.

> When Evans was killed ... Septimus, far from showing any emotion or recognizing that here was the end of a friendship, congratulated himself upon feeling very little and very reasonably.

[1] *A Writer's Diary*, October 14, 1922, p. 52.

This initial failure remains in the foreground of his awareness as 'real'; and his distorted view of reality gathers strength as his madness deepens. He has failed to bring the depth of his emotion to the surface—has failed, that is, to look at *himself* without fear, to face the terror of his love. The result is a loss of self—which for Virginia Woolf, *means* madness. In *The Waves*, for example, a character describes her precarious moments of near-madness in terms of lost identity.

> I came to the puddle. I could not cross it. Identity failed me. We are nothing, I said, and fell. . . . I returned very painfully, drawing myself back into my body over the grey, cadaverous space of the puddle.

So Lucrezia Warren Smith thinks, 'He was not Septimus now'. The distinction between himself and the world is blurred (ironically, Dr Bradshaw advises him to 'take an interest in things outside himself'); he becomes the not-self.

> His body was macerated until only the nerve fibres were left. It was spread like a veil upon a rock. . . . He lay very high, on the back of the world. The earth thrilled beneath him. Red flowers grew through his flesh; their stiff leaves rustled by his head.

Septimus' madness, therefore, stems from a lack of self-recognition which, by the time we meet him, has become incurable. Despite its false premise, however, his is 'the madness of vital truth' in one sense, and thus pertinent to Mrs Dalloway, the 'sane' member of the pair. Septimus has recognized certain necessities evaded by Clarissa, or perhaps never encountered by her. His idea that he cannot feel is false; but his reaction to this supposed fact is true. The failure becomes 'an appalling crime': 'the sin for which human nature had condemned him to death; that he did not feel'. As a result of this intuition, Septimus is burdened with guilt and haunted by the dead man.

> He sang. Evans answered from behind the tree. The dead were in Thessaly, Evans sang, among the orchids. . . .
> 'For God's sake don't come!' Septimus cried out. For he could not look upon the dead.

The key to our understanding of the parallel plot, and therefore of the novel, is in Septimus' response to his guilt. Lost among his fears and delusions, he nevertheless has accepted the consequence of them. He has recognized the seriousness of his 'failure', and in the end he executes the severe penalty for it upon himself. Peter Walsh had thought of some undefined failure in Mrs Dalloway as 'the death of her soul'; Septimus' emotional paralysis causes, though indirectly, the death of his body.

In these two deaths—the potential death of Clarissa's soul, the actual death of Septimus—the two strands of *Mrs Dalloway* come together. Virginia Woolf tells us in her preface that 'Mrs Dalloway was originally to kill herself, or perhaps merely to die at the end of the party'. With the invention and intervention of Septimus, this climax becomes unnecessary. He is a surrogate for Clarissa, so that she need die only in imagination, just as Conrad's captain need not commit an actual murder, but participates in bloodshed and guilt through the secret sharer. Clarissa's vivid physical realization of Septimus' death identifies her with him, so that she herself is saved. She, unlike Septimus, has been able to 'look upon the dead'.

He had thrown himself from a window. Up had flashed the ground; through him, blundering, bruising, went the rusty spikes. There he lay with a thud, thud, thud in his brain, and then a suffocation of blackness.

It is 'her punishment', she reflects, thus to participate in death, and at the same time to be helpless, 'forced to stand here in her evening dress'. It is also, however, her reward; for at the moment of participation she rises to a pitch of intense life—'nothing could be slow enough; nothing last too long'. Clarissa, being 'sane', has *felt* the death of Septimus consciously, as he could not feel the death of Evans; she will, therefore, be refreshed, not haunted, by the dead. 'He made her feel the beauty, made her feel the fun.'

It would be a mistake to burden Clarissa, or Virginia Woolf's intention, with over-weighted notions of guilt and redemption. The suggestions of Mrs Dalloway's weaknesses are very slight; they remain, except for the sentences about her 'failure' toward her husband, more or less vague in content. We are not to look for any positive act or definite transgression that demands expiation. Clarissa's situation is, once more, that of the hero in *The Secret Sharer*. She and the captain have both reached a point in their lives where a future course is to be decided; there is potentiality for growth or for withering of the self. The soul hangs in the balance of life and death, though the full extent of the predicament is obscured for the protagonists themselves. Into this delicate situation step the two secret sharers who, each by an act of violence, reveal an unseen depth of personality to the main characters. A current of sympathy flows out from Mrs Dalloway and from the captain, putting them in contact at once with the disorderly springs of life in another soul, and with certain irrational impulses—murderous or suicidal—in their own. Both 'doubles' cease to exist at the moment when the dominant selves are completed. . . .

. . . [Clarissa] thinks of the 'awful fear' in 'the depths of her heart': fear of death, and recognition of its intimate relation with life; fear of living itself, fear of feeling. Clarissa realizes, too, that there is a core of integrity in the ego that must be kept intact at all costs.

A thing there was that mattered; a thing, wreathed about with chatter, defaced, obscured in her own life, let drop every day in corruption, lies, chatter. This he had preserved.

In comprehending Septimus' death—he has 'plunged holding his treasure'—Clarissa herself discovers her own identity and becomes whole. She is once more, in imagination, the diver who plunges into the darkening, brightening sea to find the reality beneath the surface. The self sees itself in the mirror of another self; and out of 'communication', shared feeling, 'the embrace of death', the ego is paradoxically located and revealed. Clarissa has triumphantly evaded, in this moment of communion, 'the agonized individuality of the lost and separated souls in Hell',[2] at the same time, she has seen the value and meaning of the 'treasure', individuality, winning out over all its fears and failures.

The actual moment of revelation forms part of the brilliant climactic episode with which the novel ends—the party. Its foundations have been laid deep within the earlier sections. The Shakespearean phrases, 'If it were now to die,' and 'Fear no more' are recurrent motifs, repeated by Septimus shortly before his suicide, and by Mrs Dalloway at the end of the book when she accepts the gift of his death. This repetition marks the convergence of the two deaths, literal and figurative. . . .

From 'The Secret Sharer in *Mrs Dalloway*', *Accent*, Vol. 16, 1956, pp. 235–51 (244–9).

[2] Francis Fergusson, *Dante's Drama of the Mind*, Princeton, 1953, p. 198.

IRENE SIMON

Some Images in *Mrs Dalloway*

... After her walk through London, Clarissa comes home and enters
the hall 'as cool as a vault'; she feels 'like a nun who has left the
world and feels fold round her the familiar veils and the response to
old devotions' (p. 33). The image implies the religious feeling, the
sense of offering and thankfulness; it implies a serenity and acceptance
of life which gives value to the world she has just left. This is a
moment of peace at the centre of the whirling world. But the peace is
soon shattered by 'the shock of Lady Bruton asking Richard to lunch
without her' (p. 34). The cool vault becomes a tower, the nun withdraws
from the world into the emptiness at the heart of life (p. 35), solitude
becomes isolation, and virginity is no longer equated with purity but
with coldness, with the fear of giving oneself away. Yet devotion and
isolation, purity and coldness must be taken together to arrive at the
meaning of life as Clarissa sees it. The bed with the sheets stretched
tight across it becomes a symbol for the separation of the individual
as opposed to the moments of sudden revelation, when the world comes
closer. The moment of revelation is presented in such terms as to
suggest a kind of mystical experience. It therefore seems as if the nun's
seclusion and her coldness, the attic room and the narrow bed were
conditions of the momentary illuminations, as if withdrawing 'into the
world of perpetual solitude' were the necessary preparation for the final
coming together.

Later in the day, remembering that Peter criticizes her for her
parties, that Richard thinks it foolish of her to get excited over them,
she realizes that they are wrong, and, 'lying on the sofa, cloistered' she
says that her parties are an offering, though she wonders: an offering
to whom? (pp. 134–5). Thus, more than a hundred pages later, here
is the image of the nun and her devotion, even with the same
scepticism that had made her exclaim in the morning that 'not for a
moment did she believe in God' (p. 33). It is probably because of this
scepticism that Virginia Woolf can use this image only sparingly, and
turns to the waves and the sea to suggest the twofold movement.

The image appears already in the opening sentences. When
Clarissa leaves her house, the early morning air is fresh 'as if issued
to children on a beach', and she *plunges* into it as when she stepped
out into the garden at Bourton. The solemnity of the morning at
Bourton is later transferred to the pause in the traffic and to the hush
before Big Ben strikes. The flow of people and of carriages through

Westminster brings to Clarissa the same excitement and awe as diving into a strange element, so that the love and fear of the everflowing life around her, the wish to be taken into it and the fear of being swallowed by it, are suggested at this early stage in the novel. Yet there is also the suggestion that this exciting pageant is a vain show, that Clarissa's absorption in the life around her, as later on her love of parties and of assembling, leaves unsatisfied a deeper desire in her. Even while immersed in the flow, she seems to be groping for the 'still point of the turning world'. Just as the moment of June is an intersection of past and present, so time and timelessness intersect, and even Big Ben's 'leaden circles dissolve in the air'.

Clarissa loves the divine vitality that makes people move about and lifts the leaves in the Park on its *waves,* as she had loved dancing and riding. The image of the waves, first brought in to express the freshness of the morning air, expands to contain the 'waves of divine vitality'; being firmly established, it can endow a mere statement with a weight of significance far beyond the actual words: 'To dance, to ride, she had adored all that' (p. 9). Properly speaking, this is no image, but who shall say now where image and statement of fact can be divided from each other? It is just the purpose of Virginia Woolf to abolish the distinction between dream and reality; she effects this by mixing images with gestures, thoughts with impressions, visions with pure sensations, and by presenting them as mirrored on a consciousness. As a consequence, almost everything becomes an image projected on a screen.

By the time Clarissa reaches the Park Gates, the memory of Peter Walsh impinges more and more on her thoughts, and this brings to the fore the other theme, her sense of loneliness and of being an outsider. Peter had often scolded her for her coldness; now as she watches the taxicabs, she has a sense of 'being far out to sea and alone'. The image derives from the actual situation, but renders more than a sensation. Its connection with the plunge into the morning air and the fear of being lost in the waves relates it to the basic image developed from the start, and leads on to the incident she remembers: of once throwing a shilling into the Serpentine.

As incidents and persons float up in her memory, so she may now imagine surviving on the ebb and flow of things, here in the streets of London. There comes the consoling thought that we are part of everything and live in each other. By now, the image of the sea, the waves, the flux, has developed into a symbol of life; the fear of loneliness and the fear of being lost in the flux, the love of the flux and the love of independent existence, the twofold movement of merging and separating, of existing individually and being annihilated, are subsumed in the image, which, thanks to its ambivalence, can be used to express both aspects of the theme.

Whenever things come together and harmonize, Clarissa feels

secure as if borne up on a wave, lifted on its crest, submerged by it; when the wave falls, leaving the body on the beach, the heart is at peace. Thus, in the flower-shop, she feels 'as if this beauty, this scent, this colour, and Miss Pym liking her, trusting her, were a wave which she let flow over her ... and it lifted her up and up' (p. 16). When she sits in her room, mending her dress, quiet descends on her. 'So on a summer's day waves collect, overbalance, and fall; collect and fall; and the whole world seems to be saying "that is all" more and more ponderously, until even the heart in the body which lies in the sun on the beach says too, that is all. Fear no more, says the heart. Fear no more, says the heart, committing its burden to some sea, which sighs collectively for all sorrows, and renews, begins, collects, lets fall' (pp. 44–5). Thus, committing one's burden to the sea allays the fear of the sun. The phrase from the dirge recurs several times through Clarissa's rêverie and it is echoed in Septimus' nightmare, thus linking the worlds of 'the sane and the insane', as Virginia Woolf called it in her diary (October 14, 1922).

Sometimes the sea appears as a dangerous element and the individual as lost in the midst of it, fearing to be carried away by it. This happens in moments of separation, when the self seems to be threatened. These moments come and go, as the waves collect and fall, for there are 'tides in the body', and memories float up or sink. Like the traffic, the mind ebbs and flows, the train of thoughts or impressions moves rhythmically from past to present, from joy to sorrow, and man is borne by the waves or left on the beach. The image of the sea and the waves is fundamental to this kind of composition, and very often, as in the passage quoted, the very sentences mould themselves on the movement of the waves.

Clarissa's 'double', the shell-shocked Septimus, is haunted by the same fear and love; he is at once relieved and appalled by his loneliness; he, too, has his revelations and tries to communicate. He is repeatedly presented as a drowned sailor on a rock, far out at sea; he has gone under the sea and has been dead, and yet is now alive, and he feels himself drawing to the shore of life (p. 77). He sees the trees of the Park rising and falling like waves, and to him the sun is now terrifying, now gentle. All these link the two characters and their search for meaning. The same peace descends on him when he lies on the sofa as when Clarissa sews quietly in her room. His thoughts at this moment are a variation on Clarissa's dream of waves collecting and falling; they embrace the same elements, and end on the same comforting note: 'Fear no more, says the heart in the body; fear no more' (pp. 153–4). As Clarissa muses on his suicide, the words she had read that morning in the shop-window once more recur to her: 'Fear no more the heat of the sun' (p. 204).

The phrase recurs to link the parts, and implies that the sun is the enemy. Yet again the image is ambivalent, for sometimes the heat of the sun is kind and gentle, whether to Peter in the Park, or to Septimus at peace on the shore of the world, or about to kill himself. . . .

From 'Some Aspects of Virginia Woolf's Imagery', *English Studies*, Vol. 41, 1960, pp.180–96 (184–7).

JOHN HAWLEY ROBERTS

'Vision and Design' in Virginia Woolf

The fact that Roger Fry and Virginia Woolf were friends and colleagues in the realm of art needs no demonstration. Not only were they closely associated for many years as members of 'the Bloomsbury Group', but the Hogarth Press, established by the Woolfs in Tavistock Square, published some of Fry's essays. After Fry's death in 1934, it was Virginia Woolf who, at the request of Fry's sister, became his biographer. This portrait of the critic was undertaken, says Margery Fry in the 'Foreword' addressed to Mrs Woolf, as a result of 'one of those discussions upon the methods of the arts which illuminated his long and happy friendship with you'.

That Fry and Mrs Woolf, then, discussed 'the methods of the arts' is perfectly clear. But no one has yet raised the question as to whether or not any of Fry's critical ideas, as expressed in such essays as those collected in *Vision and Design* (1920) and *Transformations* (1926) or in the *Cézanne* monograph (1927), were in any way incorporated in Mrs Woolf's work. An examination of Fry's writings seems to me to indicate that some such influence did exist. I believe that an understanding of Fry's theories will illuminate one's reading of Virginia Woolf, particularly *Mrs Dalloway* and *To the Lighthouse*, to which novels the scope of this paper will be limited because they were done at the time when Fry and Mrs Woolf were most closely associated and because they are, it seems to me, the most striking and effective results of the influence I shall hope to demonstrate.

Any examination of Mrs Woolf's writings almost inevitably begins with her essay *Mr Bennett and Mrs Brown* (1924), in which she repudiated the realism of Bennett, Galsworthy, and Wells then in vogue and the sociological implications of their novels. The true novel, she insisted, must be self-contained and not lead to such external actions as joining a society or writing a cheque. Roger Fry in 'An Essay in Aesthetics' (originally published in the *New Quarterly*, 1909, and re-issued in *Vision and Design*, 1920) made it clear that for him art differs from life in that it requires no responsive deeds. 'In real life,' he said, 'we must ... cultivate those emotions which lead to useful action, and we are bound to appraise emotions according to the resultant action. ... But art appreciates emotion in and for itself.' This self-contained quality of art—all art, including the novel—was, I believe, one of Mrs Woolf's objectives. Her symbol for this idea is the now famous Mrs Brown, travelling through space and time in a railway carriage. Mrs Brown is what the art of fiction should try to communicate. She is, according to Mrs Woolf's label, 'the spirit we live by, life itself', a kind of inner essence rather than an external reality. She is, seen negatively, the repudiation of photographic and sociologically documentary realism. And she is, perhaps, an answer to the question Fry asked somewhat peevishly as early as the first Post-Impressionistic Exhibition in London (1910), why no English novelist took his art seriously. 'Why were they all engrossed in childish problems of photographic representation?' 'Literature,' he remarked, 'was suffering from a plethora of old clothes. Cézanne and Picasso had shown the way; writers should fling representation to the winds and follow suit.'[1]

Mrs Woolf seems to have tried to follow this advice. She did 'fling representation to the winds', and along with it, the established notion of plot. What is left, or rather, what is substituted for photographic representation and plot? I should like to suggest that what Cézanne and Picasso did in the art of painting, as explained by Roger Fry, Mrs Woolf attempted to do in the art of the novel.

What did these painters accomplish? What does art attempt? Fry's long contemplation of these problems led him to certain conclusions about the nature of all art and of the artists who serve it. His study of the group he called the Post-Impressionists taught him to conceive of art as 'depending for its effect solely on the relations of forms and colours, irrespective of what the forms and colours might represent'.[2] He attacked the theory that our recognition of the idea in a painting, its literary meaning or its dramatic and associative content, is bound up with the value of the form. When in 1920, Fry re-issued his Giotto essay, first published in 1901, he remarked in a footnote that he was 'inclined to disagree wherever in this article there appears the assumption not only that the dramatic idea may have inspired the artist to the creation of his form, but that the value of the form for us is bound up with the recognition of the dramatic idea. It now seems to me possible by a more searching analysis of our experience in front of a work of art to disentangle our reaction to pure form from our reaction to its implied associated ideas.'

Dissecting his 'experience in front of a work of art', he asked himself, 'what is the source of the affecting quality of certain systems of formal design for those who are sensitive to pure form?' And he found the answer, first, in the pleasure we take 'in the recognition of order, of inevitability in relations'. The more complex the relationship, the greater, he believed, is the delight we experience. But in all cases the basic reaction to works of art, as he was to express it a little later on,

<hr />

[1] Virginia Woolf, *Roger Fry*, pp. 164, 172.
[2] Kenneth Clark, Introduction to *Roger Fry: Last Lectures*, p. xiii.

is 'a reaction to a relation and not to sensations or objects or persons or events'. As Kenneth Clark put it in his Introduction to Fry's *Last Lectures*, 'Certain forms agree, and our joy is not in the forms themselves, but in their agreement.'

If we read *Mrs Dalloway* in the light of these remarks, we discover that the novel asks us to respond to the positive-negative relationship, the polarity, of Clarissa Dalloway and Septimus Smith, who, Mrs Woolf tells us in the preface to the Modern Library edition of the novel, are 'one and the same person'. They are not separate and individualized characters, but opposite phases of an idea of life itself. Their reality consists not of themselves as persons, but of their relationship to each other as forms. True artists, said Fry, 'do not seek to give what can, after all, be but a pale reflex of actual appearance, but to arouse the conviction of a new and definite reality' (*Roger Fry*, p. 177).

It is just such a vivid appeal that the Clarissa-Septimus combination makes. Our 'joy' in the novel consists in our recognition of the rightness of this basic design, that is, of the way in which Clarissa and Septimus complement each other, Clarissa's elementary love of life matching Septimus's repudiation of it. The two emotions complete each other to form a whole; one attitude cannot, within the limits of the novel, exist without the other. It is in this way that Clarissa and Septimus become 'one and the same person'. Their union, moreover, is created with a subtlety which, as it reveals itself to the reader, gives shading and complexity to their relationship. The Shakespearean refrain 'Fear no more the heat of the sun', which enters Clarissa's mind on p. 12 of the novel as she stands before Hatchards' window and which, in spite of her acceptance of life, asserts her capacity for fear and sorrow, reappears twice (pp. 34 and 45) before it becomes a part, on p. 154, of Septimus's thought, where it ironically reassures him just before his suicide. Even at the moment of his death, p. 164, he shares with Clarissa her love of life: 'He did not want to die. Life was good.' And then comes the refrain, modulated in its form: 'The sun was hot'. These four words, reminding us as they do of the song that has been running through Clarissa's mind, bring the two personalities together and reveal the fact that they are two expressions of the same thing, opposites, each of which nevertheless shares in the quality of the other.

Joining with the Shakespearean refrain and helping to unite Clarissa and Septimus is the image that likens life to a coin. When it first appears, there is nothing to indicate what use Mrs Woolf is going to make of it. Nor is it in its first manifestation a completed simile; rather, it comes before us merely as a phrase—like a phrase in music announced briefly, tentatively, and then allowed to wait for fuller development later on. We first hear it on p. 11, just a few lines before the Shakespearean verse also appears for the first time. Clarissa is thinking of the delight she takes in all the objects around her: cabs, people, the wagons plodding past to market. And suddenly come the words, 'She remembered once throwing a shilling into the Serpentine'. Immediately, associated with this memory and with her love of life, comes the opposed emotion which accepts death as a consolation. To this, in the next sentence, is added the feeling 'that somehow in the streets of London, on the ebb and flow of things, here, there, she survived ... she being part, she was positive ... of people she had never met'. Thus a highly complicated set of feelings and thoughts is established: life, death, the shilling thrown into the Serpentine, her sense of being merged with unknown persons, and—finally—the words 'Fear no more the heat of the sun'. Some two hundred pages later Septimus dies. He 'flung himself vigorously, violently down on to Mrs Filmer's area railings'. Perhaps the reader at this point is not yet ready to connect the throwing away of a shilling and the flinging away of a life; but when the news of Septimus's death reaches Clarissa at her party, p. 202, and she hears that he threw himself from a window, she immediately recalls that 'she had once thrown a shilling into the Serpentine, never anything more. But he had flung it away.' And she sees in his death 'an attempt to communicate; people feeling the impossibility of reaching the centre which, mystically, evaded them; closeness drew apart; rapture faded, one was alone. There was an embrace in death.' Intuitively she has shared with Septimus his need for death. And almost at once (p. 204), hearing the clock strike and remembering for the last time the words 'Fear no more', she recognizes the fact that she feels 'somehow very like him—the young man who had killed himself. She felt glad that he had done it; thrown it away.' Thus the words are woven. The reader, with delight, hears the echoes and apprehends the basic design, the relationship between Clarissa and Septimus which is in itself the novel's meaning.

But this analysis, before it is complete, must include still one more device—that is, Mrs Woolf's use of the little old lady who lives opposite Clarissa. We first see her on p. 140, where she becomes for Clarissa, 'who watched out of the window the old lady opposite climbing upstairs', a symbol of the privacy of the soul, the central mystery of life that is summed up in the phrase, 'here was one room; there another'. Later when in the scene already described, Clarissa hears of Septimus's death, she again looks out through the window and exclaims, 'Oh, but how surprising!' for 'in the room opposite the old lady stared straight at her!' And when, in a moment, the old lady puts out her light, it is then that Clarissa, to the accompaniment of the clock and the Shakespearean refrain, feels that she and Septimus are one. Now this little old lady not only exists for Clarissa, but actually has her counterpart for Septimus in the form of the old gentleman who, at the very instant that Septimus flings himself down on the area railings, suddenly descends the staircase opposite and stares at him (p. 164). This set of connected contrasts—the old lady going upstairs, the old man coming down; the one opposite Clarissa, the other opposite

Septimus; the one staring at Clarissa, the other staring at Septimus—
this set of connected contrasts makes a balance of detail that supports
and strengthens the fundamental dichotomy. The reader's response
to the whole is very much like that of one who standing before a
painting begins to see, as Fry would see, how this mass necessarily
balances that, how this line repeats, with a difference, that one, how a
highlight here inevitably answers a shadow there, how, in other words,
the meaning of the picture lies in our discovery of the fact that the
forms agree. . . .

The next novel was *To the Lighthouse*, published in 1927. This
book is, I believe, another attempt to make form and meaning one.
And in it we have the helpful and significant figure of Lily Briscoe, the
artist, whose ideas about art are identical with those of Roger Fry. . . .

. . . For Fry the artistic experience is unlike any other because it is
a reaction to a relation and not to sensations or objects or persons or
events. But literature, he admitted, is not such a clear case as painting
or architecture or music. The novel, with its loose structure, can have
within a single work criticism of life, moral or religious or social
teaching, and manners, any one of which may have been the immediate
cause for the writing of the novel. Nevertheless, Fry insists, if there is
any aesthetic effect, it does not arise from these ulterior purposes but
from the 'creation of structures which have for us a feeling of reality,
and . . . these structures are self-contained, self-sufficing, and not to
be valued by their reference to what lies outside'.

It seems to him true, furthermore, that, at least in painting, however
strong the appeal of the subject matter may be, the part of one's
response which has been aroused by the subject quickly fades, while
'what remains, what never grows less or evaporates, are the feelings
dependent on the purely formal relations'. In spite of the fact that the
greater part of humanity, he admits, responds more readily to objects,
persons, and ideas—in other words to the relatively transient associative emotions of a work of art, nevertheless the permanent values
accrue to that lesser group that directs its attention 'to the completest
relationship of all the parts within the system'. He believes that
'these systems of formal relations . . . have a curious vitality and
longevity, whereas those works in which appeal is made chiefly to the
associated ideas . . . rarely survive the generation for whose pleasure
they were made. . . . The result is that the accumulated and inherited
artistic treasure of mankind is made up almost entirely from those
works in which formal design is the predominant consideration.'

I have dwelt thus at length on the concept of formal relationship
and the permanent satisfaction that derives from it (rather than from
associative emotions) because it seems to me that in *To the Lighthouse*
Mrs Woolf is dealing with those two closely connected ideas. Although
this novel tells a story, the story element is slight in the extreme. Our
attention is focused on the problem of relationship, simultaneously

E

human and formal. That is to say, *To the Lighthouse* discusses both human relationship and formal relationship and, moreover, testifies to the truth that permanent values lie not in the one, but in the other: not in life but in art.

Mrs Ramsay, so far as human matters are concerned, attempts in the first section of the novel to bring about something beautiful and permanent in the contacts among the people gathered for the summer in the Hebrides. Acutely aware of 'the inadequacy of human relation-ships, that the most perfect was flawed' (pp. 66, 69), she suffers from her recognition of her husband's vanity, hopes for the happy marriage of her daughter Prue, manoeuvres to bring about the wedding of Paul and Minta, seeks to protect her youngest son James from his father's peevishness, often resorts to exaggerations of statement and emotion in an effort to create order, does good works in the village, knows she is accused of meddling and interfering, and has to admit, in her bleaker moments, 'that she felt this thing that she called life terrible, hostile, and quick to pounce on you if you gave it a chance. There were the eternal problems: suffering, death, the poor' (p. 96).

Her efforts fail. Her husband remains a confused mixture of egoism and unworldliness; Prue dies in childbirth; Paul and Minta do not find happiness together; James hates his father. Even her transcendent beauty, so often stressed in the novel, is, after all, only physical. And when Mrs Ramsay dies, that great beauty, as a physical attribute, dies with her.

But on at least two occasions before her death she gets a glimpse of a solution to the inadequacies of human relationships. At one point, seeing that the signs by which we know each other are 'simply childish', she acknowledges the need for silence and isolation: 'All the being and the doing, expansive, glittering, vocal, evaporated; and one shrank, with a sense of solemnity, to being oneself, a wedge-shaped core of darkness, something invisible to others ... and this self having shed its attachments was free for the strangest adventures. When life sank down for a moment, the range of experience seemed limitless' (pp. 99–100). This 'wedge-shaped core of darkness' is a repetition of that abstract pattern, the 'triangular purple shape', which Lily Briscoe, who will be discussed in a moment, has seen as the way to paint Mrs Ramsay. And at another point during the dinner scene, she feels that when the candles are lighted, the faces around the table are 'com-posed' (that is, made into a composition), because the candlelight has shut off the watery, wavering outside world and permitted a sense of order to establish itself (p. 151).

On both these occasions the factor that solves the eternal problem of human relationships is a formal factor substituted for the human ego. And in each instance the result is a design or it is a composition in which individual personalities give way to an agreement among formal parts. 'Not as oneself,' she said, 'did one find rest ever ... but as a wedge of darkness. Losing personality, one lost the fret, the hurry, the stir; and there rose to her lips always some exclamation of triumph over life when things came together in peace' (p. 100).

But however true these intuitive glimpses into the triumph of art over life may be for Mrs Ramsay, it is Lily Briscoe, herself an artist, who makes the complete discovery. Lily, like Mrs Ramsay, is trying to create order; but her medium is paint and canvas, not human lives. She is vividly aware of the importance of mass, line, and colour; most of all she can see the essential shape beneath surfaces. But her difficulty is to transfer this design to the canvas. In her picture of Mrs Ramsay reading to James in the window, Mrs Ramsay is 'a triangular purple shape' (p. 84). When Mr Bankes objects that it does not look human, Lily replies that far from attempting a likeness or representation, she is trying to balance a lightness here with a darkness there. And even Mr Bankes begins to see that mother and child can be reduced 'to a purple shadow without irreverence'. He begins to understand that the problem is 'one of the relations of masses' and that the issue at stake is, as Lily points out, 'how to connect this mass on the right hand with that on the left' (pp. 85–6). This technical puzzle, discussed by these characters in the very language of Roger Fry, occupies Lily's mind throughout the novel. During dinner it comes to her that by moving the tree nearer the middle she can not only avoid an awkward space but also gain the unity she is striving for, and she moves a salt cellar on the table to remind herself to move the tree. As the dinner scene continues, Lily, encountering Tansley's egocentric feeling of inferiority, begins to speculate on the difficulty of all human relationships—particularly those between men and women—when the sight of the salt cellar reminds her that she may perhaps be able after all to solve the aesthetic mystery. 'Her spirits rose so high at the thought of painting tomorrow that she laughed out loud at what Mr Tansley was saying' (p. 144).

But it is ten years—not one day—before Lily returns to the canvas. The problem of life (human relationships) and the problem of art (formal relationships) have not yet been solved. Mrs Ramsay is dead. Mr Ramsay is more cranky and vain than ever. The house is 'full of unrelated passions'. But Lily turns to her painting once more—and once more is 'drawn out of gossip, out of living, out of community with people, into the presence of this formidable ancient enemy of hers,'—the battle with form (pp. 244–50).

In a fashion not unlike that experienced by Mrs Ramsay, Lily sheds attachments; she loses 'consciousness of outer things, of her name and her personality and her appearance' and in a kind of trance she begins to remember Mrs Ramsay as one who 'resolved everything into simplicity', as one who 'brought together this and that and then this' in such a way that what she created became complete, affecting Lily, she says, 'like a work of art'. Mrs Ramsay, at this moment, becomes for

Lily the permanence of form in human relationships: 'In the midst of chaos there was shape; this eternal passing and flowing . . . was struck into stability.'

The lasting values in life and art are not, then, in the shifting details on the surface of things but rather in the formal and permanent pattern that both life and art must try to achieve. What art attempts (even though the goal may not be reached) remains forever. What Mrs Ramsay attempted during her days of action (even though she did not succeed) is the final truth. Death does not destroy it. And Lily at last realizes that when space takes on form and empty flourishes take on shape—then the answer to the mystery of art and life has been found, deeply rooted, as Fry would say, in our love of order.

At this moment, as the novel draws to its close, Mr Ramsay and James and Cam reach the lighthouse. They reach it just as Mr Ramsay, at last freed from his egocentrism (the enemy of human order) praises James. At this moment, Lily, knowing intuitively that the boating party has landed, finishes her picture. She draws a line in the centre; the design is complete. She has had, she says, 'her vision'.

It is not altogether accidental, perhaps, that the last word of the novel is the word 'vision', a word so important to Roger Fry that he used it in his title *Vision and Design*. Mrs Woolf implies in her biography that the word 'vision' stands for the emotions, balanced by the word 'design', which stands for the intellect. That is, what the artist sees and what he feels about what he sees become a work of art when the inner form has been translated to the canvas—when the significance of the vision is communicated not in the language of surface representation but in the language of design. This is the lesson that Lily Briscoe learns in *To the Lighthouse*. And this is also the truth about life, the 'meaning' of which lies not on its surface but in the deeper pattern seen when 'the self has shed its attachments'. Then —and then only—'things come together in peace'.

As to the problem of its own form, *To the Lighthouse* structurally is like a pool which narcisstically reflects its theme. Here again, as in *Mrs Dalloway*, we have time and space creating the frame within which the 'psychological values' find their final relationship. The rhythm of time and the rhythm of the sea beat through the pages. Much is made of colour. With both time and colour there is a deliberate use of blur. Within the first twenty-six pages various episodes fade into one another and out again in the manner of montage in the cinema. The result is that we find ourselves confronting simultaneously a particular evening in the present and a number of other related moments. Present, past, and future become one, in which fusion the pattern alone becomes important. Similarly, Part III (The Lighthouse) is connected structurally with Part I (The Window) by means of the transitional section (Time Passes), and Lily's mind, going back through time, at last completes the spiritual design, just as by drawing the line in the centre she at last finishes her picture. Past and present have become one. This unity is itself the novel's meaning: Mrs Ramsay, though dead, still lives, not in the beauty of her flesh, which, like all merely associative emotions, must—according to Fry—dissolve and fade, but as the means by which order is brought out of chaos,—as the uniquely aesthetic principle which brings to a complete relationship all the parts within the system.

From ' "Vision and Design" in Virginia Woolf', in *P.M.L.A.*, Vol. 61, 1946, pp. 835–47 (835–9, 842–7). Some footnotes have been omitted.

DAVID DAICHES

Symbolic Pattern in
To the Lighthouse

...The characters in *To the Lighthouse* are carefully arranged in
their relation to each other, so that a definite symbolic pattern emerges.
Mr Ramsay, the professor of philosophy, who made one original
contribution to thought in his youth and has since been repeating and
elaborating it without being able to see through to the ultimate implications of his system; his wife, who knows more of life in an unsyste-
matic and intuitive way, who has no illusions ('There was no treachery
too base for the world to commit; she knew that. No happiness lasted;
she knew that.') yet presides over her family with a calm and com-
petent efficiency; Lily Briscoe, who refuses to get married and tries
to express her sense of reality in terms of colour and form; Charles
Tansley, the aggressive young philosopher with an inferiority complex;
old Mr Carmichael, who dozes unsocially in the sun and eventually
turns out to be a lyric poet; Minta Doyle and Paul Rayley, the undis-
tinguished couple whom Mrs Ramsay gently urges into a not too
successful marriage—each character has a very precise function in
this carefully organized story. The lighthouse itself, standing lonely
in the midst of the sea, is a symbol of the individual who is at once a
unique being and a part of the flux of history. To reach the lighthouse
is, in a sense, to make contact with a truth outside oneself, to surrender
the uniqueness of one's ego to an impersonal reality. Mr Ramsay,
who is an egotist constantly seeking applause and encouragement from
others, resents his young son's enthusiasm for visiting the lighthouse,
and only years later, when his wife has died and his own life is
almost worn out, does he win this freedom from self—and it is
significant that Virginia Woolf makes Mr Ramsay escape from his
egotistic preoccupations for the first time just before the boat finally
reaches the lighthouse. Indeed, the personal grudges nourished by
each of the characters fall away just as they arrive; Mr Ramsay ceases
to pose with his book and breaks out with an exclamation of admiration
for James's steering; James and his sister Cam lose their resentment
at their father's way of bullying them into this expedition and cease
hugging their grievances: 'What do you want? they both wanted to
ask. They both wanted to say, Ask us anything and we will give it you.
But he did not ask them anything.' And at the moment when they
land, Lily Briscoe and old Mr Carmichael, who had not joined the

expedition, suddenly develop a mood of tolerance and compassion for mankind, and Lily has the vision which enables her to complete her picture.

There is a colour symbolism running right through the book. When Lily Briscoe is wrestling unsuccessfully with her painting, in the first part of the book, she sees the colours as 'bright violet and staring white', but just as she achieves her final vision at the book's conclusion, and is thus able to complete her picture, she notices that the lighthouse 'had melted away into a blue haze'; and though she sees the canvas clearly for a second before drawing the final line, the implication remains that this blurring of colours is bound up with her vision. Mr Ramsay, who visualizes the last, unattainable, step in his philosophy as glimmering *red* in the distance, is contrasted with the less egotistical Lily, who works with blues and greens, and with Mrs Ramsay, who is indicated on Lily's canvas as 'a triangular purple shape'. Red and brown appear to be the colours of individuality and egotism, while blue and green are the colours of impersonality. Mr Ramsay, until the very end of the book, is represented as an egotist, and his colour is red or brown; Lily is the impersonal artist, and her colour is blue; Mrs Ramsay stands somewhere between, and her colour is purple.[1] The journey to the lighthouse is the journey from egotism to impersonality. . . .

From Chapter 4 of *Virginia Woolf*, New Directions, Norfolk, Connecticut, 1942, pp. 86–8.

[1] There is a beautiful example of this colour symbolism on pp. 279–80: 'Wherever she happened to be, painting, here, in the country or in London, the vision would come to her, and her eyes, half closing, sought something to base her vision on. She looked down the railway carriage, the omnibus; took a line from shoulder or cheek; looked at the windows opposite; at Piccadilly, lamp-strung in the evening. All had been part of the fields of death. But always something—it might be a face, a voice, a paper boy crying *Standard, News*—thrust through, snubbed her, waked her, required and got in the end an effort of attention, so that the vision must be perpetually remade. Now again, moved as she was by some instinctive need of distance and blue, she looked at the bay beneath her, making hillocks of the blue bars of the waves, and stony fields of the purpler spaces, again she was roused as usual by something incongruous. There was a brown spot in the middle of the bay. It was a boat. Yes, she realised that after a second. But whose boat ? Mr Ramsay's boat, she replied. Mr Ramsay; the man who had marched past her, with his hand raised, aloof, at the head of a procession, in his beautiful boots, asking her for sympathy, which she had refused. The boat was now half way across the bay.'

This passage, while taking its place naturally in the development of the story, at the same time throws an important light on the earlier and later parts of the book, clarifying symbolism and enriching significance. The artist, having an 'instinctive need of . . . blue,' sees Mr Ramsay's boat as a *brown* spot on a *blue* sea. Brown is the personal colour, the egotistic colour; blue belongs to the impersonality of the artist.

Mr and Mrs Ramsay

... the title *To the Lighthouse* synthesizes and fuses the details of her novel through the highly evocative image of the lighthouse. Even before she started to write, Virginia Woolf saw the novel in terms of three parts: (1) at the drawing room window, (2) seven years pass, (3) the voyage (*A Writer's Diary*, July 20, 1925). The events in the first section, 'The Window', grow in momentum until they are submerged in the anonymous realm of nature and time in Part II, 'Time Passes', only to reappear in Part III, 'The Lighthouse', where they are echoed across the years of the middle section. The effect is to turn the two widely disparate moments of Parts I and III into a specious present. The title, then, points to the fact that the relation between the first and last sections, between 'The Window' and 'The Lighthouse', is both the form and the significance of the book.

The window in Part I is, naturally, the literal one at which Mrs Ramsay sits with her small son James, the two of them forming the subject of a painting being executed by Lily Briscoe below on the lawn. The title, however, has a much wider application. Each of the characters has his window opening on the world, and much of the first section of the novel differentiates the frames of references of Mrs Ramsay, Mr Ramsay, Lily Briscoe, the children, Charles Tansley, etc.[1] In addition to giving the view each one has from his window, Virginia Woolf, adding her own voice to the voice of the characters, bit by bit completes a view 'in' as well as 'out', in other words, a view of the viewer framed by the window. The moments of vision which occur much later in Part III must be understood as occurring within the frames supplied in Part I.

Moreover, in Part I Virginia Woolf prepares the reader to under-stand the title of Part III, 'The Lighthouse'. Beginning with an actual lighthouse which stands out in the sea, she quickly allies this real lighthouse with a spiritual one: an illuminated experience in the

---

[1] Throughout this section, various characters explicitly try to organize a coherent view of the world. Obviously Lily Briscoe in art and Mr Ramsay in philosophy are so engaged. In addition Mr Bankes pursues that science most addicted to pigeon-holing: botany; and Andrew Ramsay is gifted in the most coherent of the sciences: mathematics. Even the girls, Nancy and Rose, try to shape the chaos of materials into order, the one on the beach playing God with water and sunlight, the other in the dining room arranging flowers. Mrs Ramsay, of course, is the chief example of the individual who tries to compose human relations into patterns of significance.

past which stands up out of the waste of time and sheds its glow on the present. In addition the path the eye traverses in seeing is compared to the ray sent out by a lighthouse. Thus Lily Briscoe sees William Bankes gazing with love at Mrs Ramsay and 'looking along his beam she added to it her different ray' (p. 79). In 'The Lighthouse' by following along these various rays sent out by the lighthouses of the characters' minds, the reader not only sees what the characters see; he knows how to interpret what they see because of his knowledge of their windows on the world.

The relation between Parts I and III, therefore, goes much deeper than the surface one supplied by the trip to the lighthouse. One of the delightful ingenuities in the actual working out of the relationship occurs as a result of that discontinuity which is found to be the basic continuity of human existence. Despite Mrs Ramsay's death, Part III is a recapitulation and fulfilment of the first section; for it is James and Cam, not Mr and Mrs Ramsay, who have the visions which proceed from the 'windows' of Part I. Cam now occupies her mother's position between James and Mr Ramsay. Torn between the demands of father and brother, as her mother was between husband and son, Cam—the free-flying, heedless child exulting in speed and power in Part I—is clearly beginning to see the world from an angle very like her mother's. James at the same time is assuming the characteristics of his father. The trip to the lighthouse, therefore, offers more than an ironic comment upon the belated fulfilment of James' desire to visit the lighthouse. Similarly, the completion of Lily Briscoe's painting, another literal fulfilment of a desire initiated ten years before, supports a more personal fulfilment; for in her vision Lily attains the intimacy with Mrs Ramsay that was earlier denied her.

'Time Passes' is the necessary link between the two. The cosmic perspective which has persistently added its peculiar quality to Virginia Woolf's previous novels has now come to the fore. In context Part II performs an important technical function, giving the reader space in which to allow experience to change into memory by the alchemy of time. It wrenches the reader out of the human sphere and rinses the mind of its perpetual concern with flesh and blood before introducing the human being again in the centre of the stage.

The author's attitude toward those human beings is extremely complicated. None of their weaknesses escape her mockery and yet she displays a very real if qualified respect for them.[2] She treats Mr Ramsay's intellectual endeavours, his ascent from A to Q, as an object

---

[2] Virginia Woolf employs all the satiric techniques described by J. I. M. Stewart as Lytton Strachey's tools of the craft. He notes that Strachey's characteristic techniques for creating humour are: the use of Victorian idiom, deft focusing of incongruities and disparities, anti-climax, and the assertion of norms against which are set 'actual persuasion and activities of the subject' ("Biography", *Craft of Letters*, ed. by John Lehmann, pp. 6-25).

for amusement, but she never forgets that thought is one of the greatest fruits of civilization. When he becomes engrossed in ideas, Mr Ramsay discards personal vanity.

> It was his power, his gift, suddenly to shed all superfluities, to shrink and diminish so that he looked barer and felt sparer, even physically, yet lost none of his intensity of mind, and so to stand on his little ledge facing the dark of human experience, how we know nothing and the sea eats away the ground we stand on—that was his fate, his gift ... not only fame but even his own name was forgotten by him, he kept even in that desolation a vigilance which spared no phantom and luxuriated in no vision ... (p. 72).

It is this power that makes Mr Ramsay worthy of the respect of his colleagues and his wife. Similarly Mrs Ramsay's naive belief in marriage as the panacea for all womankind does not escape Virginia Woolf's scorn, and yet the reader is made to admire her almost divine power in human relations. She knows how to answer her husband's continual need for love and sympathy. She can rest her head on a frightened child's pillow and turn an imagined world of horrors into 'a bird's nest ... a beautiful mountain ... with valleys and flowers and bells ringing and birds singing and little goats and antelopes ...' (p. 177). She can make a prig like Charles Tansley feel happy and proud to be walking 'with a beautiful woman for the first time in his life' (p. 28), or a young booby like Paul Rayley feel he can do anything. The reader recognizes the basis of Mrs Ramsay's hold on the affections of almost all the characters in the novel. . . .

When the expedition seems so certainly to have shattered on the rocks of Mr Ramsay's truth, Mrs Ramsay builds up the world of possibilities: 'Perhaps you will wake up and find the sun shining and the birds singing.' 'Perhaps it will be fine tomorrow.' 'And even if it isn't fine tomorrow ... it will be another day.' The domestic situation ends with Mr Ramsay's loss of temper, his 'Damn you' in the face of the 'extraordinary irrationality' of her remarks. Mrs Ramsay's response to her husband's exasperation clarifies the nature of the relation between them.

> They came to her, naturally, since she was a woman, all day long with this and that; one wanting this, another that; the children were growing up; she often felt she was nothing but a sponge sopped full of human emotions. Then he said, Damn you. He said, It must rain. He said, It won't rain, and instantly a Heaven of security opened before her. There was nobody she reverenced more. She was not good enough to tie his shoe strings, she felt (pp. 54–5).

Mr Ramsay reverences her for just the opposite reason: she keeps the range of possibilities ever open. Her peculiar strength and weakness as a woman is that sense of chance, of fickleness which makes her incapable of relegating particular situations to the iron grip of general theories. She is, therefore, a guardian of human aspiration, preparing and preserving an atmosphere in which nothing is irrevocable, everything is possible.

But since it is a great strain to go on creating such a world of infinite possibilities, Mrs Ramsay is almost abjectly grateful to her husband who with masculine arrogance gives order and limit to her necessarily fluid and unbounded world. For the feminine sense of infinite possibility carries with it an imaginative burden. Mrs Ramsay is constantly aware of danger, of accidents and death, a fear which is only the other side of the coin of hope. If all is possible, one must anticipate broken arms as well as fair days. The sense of life as something hostile, an enemy capable of untold enormities, accounts for Mrs Ramsay's desire that her children never grow up.

> knowing what was before them—love and ambition and being wretched alone in dreary places—she had often the feeling, why must they grow up and lose it all? And then she said to herself, brandishing her sword at life, nonsense. They will be perfectly happy.

There resides in the core of her heart a frightening vision which rises up in her moments of solitude. The fairy tale she is reading James is the prototype of that vision: the race's ageless picture of man in a world of terrible possibilities.

> 'Then he put on his trousers and ran away like a madman,' she read. 'But outside a great storm was raging and blowing so hard that he could scarcely keep his feet; houses and trees toppled over, the mountains trembled, rocks rolled into the sea, the sky was pitch black and it thundered and lightened, and the sea came in with black waves as high as church towers and mountains, and all with white foam at the top.' (p. 97)

Mr Ramsay offers protection against the overwhelming force of these dangers. The masculine and feminine points of view enrich, support, counteract each other. The question of which is the better window on life is irrelevant. . . .

Mr and Mrs Ramsay's attitudes toward time further illustrate this difference between the masculine and feminine consciousness. When Mrs Ramsay wants to know if it is getting late, she looks into the garden where the light tells her how close it is to evening. When Mr Ramsay wants to know if it is getting late, he flicks open his watch and sees it is 'only just past seven'. He has accurate, theoretical knowledge; she has vague, immediate knowledge. The thing exists for her, the mental construct for him.

These different attitudes seriously alter the perspective of the minds in which they function. The man tends to grow unaware of the objects that are the basis of his constructs. He tends to become dry, weary, tied in knots from his constant sojourn in the area of the quintessential. Mr Ramsay's insatiable appetite for sympathy, comfort, attention results from the unappeased whole man; for his intellectual occupations require a degree of specialization that necessarily starves his senses, his emotions. That fatal sterility, which has been so poorly understood by Virginia Woolf's critics, is not a permanent attribute of men, but an 'occupational disease'. From Virginia Woolf's middle-class view of masculine occupations (generations of lawyers, dons, civil servants), men's activities are peculiarly unrestorative. Women's 'delicious fecundity' is a common gift which has been preserved by their constant contact with a world that requires a total rather than a partial response. So the man must come to the woman.

> to be taken within the circle of life, warmed and soothed, to have his senses restored to him, his barrenness made fertile, and all the rooms of the house made full of life—the drawing-room; behind the drawing-room the kitchen; above the kitchen the bedrooms; and beyond them the nurseries; they must be furnished, they must be filled with life (p. 62).

Although she inhabits a rich, living world, the woman is cut off from the wider world which might give order, coherence, enlargement to the narrower. As a result she tends to become petty, possessive, limited. Mrs Ramsay thinks Prue will be happier than Minta, because she is *her* daughter. She is willing to sacrifice Charles Tansley's happiness to Mr Ramsay's good opinion of himself because he is *her* husband. And because Mrs Ramsay is involved constantly in the petty, personal concerns of daily living, she feels used up emotionally, without any energy for her own expenditures. No wonder then that man's clear recognition of fact as distinct from emotion ('You won't finish that stocking tonight') makes him an almost godlike figure. . . .

But as Lily Briscoe perceives, these roles distort the personalities of husband and wife. Mr Ramsay persistently demands that his wife give, and she always obliges by sacrificing her will to his. The man, however, becomes enslaved by his own tyranny, seeking, imploring the consolation his vanities require. The woman becomes mildly disdainful of her lord and in her constricted world begins to feel all men are to be pitied 'as if they lacked something—women never, as if they had something' (p. 133). This pity leads her to employ on man's behalf that rare faculty women have for creating an orderly pattern out of the daily facts of existence. Never have the dangers of that power been so clearly indicated as in *To the Lighthouse*.

Why does Augustus Carmichael distrust Mrs Ramsay? Why did Minta Doyle's mother say something that reminds Mrs Ramsay of another woman's accusation that she was 'robbing her of her daughter's affections'? (p. 92). Why does Paul Rayley feel, immediately after his engagement, that he 'would go straight to Mrs Ramsay, because he felt somehow that she was the person who had made him do it'? Cut off from the wider world of action available to men, Mrs Ramsay finds no range for the exertion of her powers and inevitably employs them in personal domination. . . .

Virginia Woolf sees possibilities for humour in Mrs Ramsay's small world and limited view. She turns the matter into a physical disability; three times at least Mrs Ramsay is described as short-sighted.[3] She sees what is right in front of her: the man putting up billboards, her husband and children, the two figures immediately before her on a lawn. Deftly the deficiency in sight and the practical exertion of will are made correspondent:

> Ah, but was that not Lily Briscoe strolling along with William Bankes? She focused her short-sighted eyes upon the backs of the retreating couple. Yes, indeed it was. Did that not mean that they would marry? Yes, it must! What an admirable idea! They must marry (p. 113).

And yet it is this particular human being, Mrs Ramsay, compact of great strength and weakness, whose presence gives shape and coherence to the famous dinner party; 'And directly she went a sort of disintegration set in . . .' (p. 173). The candles, the fragrant and delicious *Boeuf en Daube,* the family, the friends, combine to form a moment in life which resembles in its beauty and completeness a work of art. That dining room becomes a lighthouse as the group grows conscious of being a party.

> Now all the candles were lit, and the faces on both sides of the table were brought nearer by the candle light, and composed, as they had not been in the twilight, into a party round a table, for the night was now shut off by panes of glass, which, far from giving any accurate view of the outside world, rippled it so strangely that here, inside the room, seemed to be order and dry land. There, outside, a reflection in which things wavered and vanished, waterily (p. 151).

[3] Her short-sightedness is connected, of course, with a virtue. She does see what is before her. Thus the first reference to this disability occurs in the description of her walk into town with Charles Tansley. Mrs Ramsay is full of excited interest in the scene around her, whereas her companion is preoccupied with his own thoughts of professional honours. She cranes forward to read the billboard announcing a circus among other things. Tansley, however, 'though they had reached the town now and were in the main street, with carts grinding past on the cobbles, still . . . went on talking about settlements and teaching, and working men, and helping our own class, and lectures . . .', until Mrs Ramsay makes him stop to look at a lovely view (p. 25). This short-sightedness also makes her very sensitive in registering slight alterations in her limited view. This particular sensitivity is most acute in respect to her husband who has been an object on whom she has fixed her short-sighted eyes these many years.

The real lighthouse of the novel, therefore, is the one which Mrs Ramsay carefully sets glowing and which illuminates a space of life even after her death. This illumination becomes a triumph of the human spirit as Virginia Woolf recounts the dead beginnings of this memorable party. The mood of utter emptiness with which the meal commences, Mrs Ramsay's sense 'of being past everything, through everything, out of everything' (p. 130), is a mood very like Mrs Dalloway's when she reads the note from Richard upon her return home. By means of formulas, of conventional chatter, Mrs Ramsay sets about lifting that gloom. As always Virginia Woolf shows what effort is required to resist the attractions of oblivion and return to life. Even Mrs Ramsay, a guardian of life, finds it difficult to summon her powers and take up the burden of living again. In her dead mood she sees the joyous meal that may occur if she takes the immense trouble to set about creating it. Virginia Woolf compares her to a sailor who 'not without weariness sees the wind fill his sail and yet hardly wants to be off again and thinks how, had the ship sunk, he would have whirled round and round and found rest on the floor of the sea' (p. 131). She rouses herself and with much effort rekindles the lighthouse, making it shine so brilliantly that ten years later Lily Briscoe, James and Cam see by its light again. . . .

From Chapter 5 of *The Three-fold Nature of Reality in the Novels of Virginia Woolf*, Mouton and Co., The Hague, 1965, pp. 111–13, 118–25. Some footnotes have been omitted.

IRENE SIMON

The Sea in *To the Lighthouse*

... Virginia Woolf uses [sea-images] to suggest opposite meanings: the
sea is both destroyer and protector; it engulfs the individual elements
and brings them together; it threatens the ordered world and creates
harmony. To Mr Ramsay, the sea is the enemy, and he defies the
flood from his spit of land. To Mrs Ramsay, the sound of the waves
can be like 'a ghostly roll of drums remorselessly beat[ing] the measure
of life', it can make her 'think of the destruction of the island and its
engulfment in the sea' and warn her that everything is ephemeral
(p. 30). But the waves falling on the beach also beat a 'measured and
soothing tattoo to her thoughts' and repeat consolingly 'I am guarding
you—I am your support' (p. 30).

Indeed the individual feels his nothingness in front of the sea,
because it seems, as Lily says, 'to outlast by a million years the gazer
and to be communing already with a sky which beholds an earth
entirely at rest' (p. 37). The indifference of nature and the survival of
the earth, whatever happens to man, will be presented in the interlude: Time Passes. To the assertive self, engulfment can mean nothing
but annihilation: that is probably the reason why to Mr Ramsay the
sea is nothing but the enemy. To those, however, who attempt to
merge, who dread separateness, it is a relief to be carried away by
the flood. So Mrs Ramsay feels 'outside that eddy' (p. 130) when things
remain separate. Yet to her also, order appears as a victory won over
the waters. When the candles are lit, the party round the table is
'composed' and seems 'to be order and dry land'; they all make a
party on an island, having 'their common cause against that fluidity out
there' (p. 152). Indeed, if life is the flux, significance and permanence
can only be achieved by such creation of order. So when the link 'that
bound things together ha[s] been cut, they *float* up there, down there,
off anyhow'; floating at random becomes an image of chaos, and the
sea is once more a symbol of disintegration.

Yet, Lily and William Bankes stroll down every evening to the break
in the hedge to look at the sea, as if 'drawn by some need'. The sea
seems to release unknown powers in them, makes them expand beyond
the limitations of self. So that in the third part, when Lily tries to grasp
her vision, she turns again and again to the sea. It is as though contemplation of the sea and the bark sailing on it brought into proper perspective the relation of time and timelessness, of individual objects
and the whole to which they belong. As David Daiches has shown,

blue is the colour of the impersonal artist, and it is the sea that enables men to reach the impersonal vision. Cam looking at the island from the boat sees it become 'steadily more distant and more peaceful' (p. 281), and her mind wanders in the underworld of waters 'where in the green light a change came over one's entire mind and one's body shone half transparent enveloped in a green cloak' (p. 281). The sea, then, reveals the luminous halo, and Lily trying to get her canvas into perspective feels as 'on a narrow plank, perfectly alone, over the sea' (p. 265). There she can satisfy her 'need of distance and blue' (p. 279), she can see things in their proper relations. Her vision is an insight into the nature of life and death, dissolution and permanence, individual being and the surrounding world. Only by maintaining the proper balance between the two terms in each pair can significant form be achieved. That is why the main images in the novel must be ambivalent symbols, for Virginia Woolf, like Lily, must achieve 'the razor edge of balance between two opposite forces' (p. 296).

The correlative of this significant form in *To the Lighthouse,* as so often in Virginia Woolf's work, is the *wave.* When Lily first tries to express her vision of the Ramsays and their world, and grasps the perfect integration of the scene, she feels 'how life, from being made up of little separate incidents which one lived one by one, became curled and whole like a wave which bore one up with it and threw one down with it, there, with a dash on the beach' (p. 76). When ecstasy bursts in Mrs Ramsay's eyes at the stroke of the lighthouse, 'waves of pure delight race over the floor of her mind' (p. 103). The mind at peace rises and falls with the sea, and the rhythm of the waves makes it lose itself and go under (p. 231). The regular beat of the waves on the beach reassures and brings peace (p. 30). Looking at the sea from a cliff top, one sees the waves shaping themselves symmetrically (p. 244). As Lily paints, she attains a dancing rhythmical movement, and the lines on her canvas image the movement of the waves (p. 244). They bring messages of peace to the shore and, when the party at last returns to the house, the waves break gently and 'the sigh of all the seas breaking in measure round the isles' soothes the sleepers (p. 220). When at last Mr Ramsay and his children are freed from their resentment, the boat sails 'buoyantly on long rocking waves . . . with an extraordinary lilt and exhilaration' (pp. 316–7) and they can hear the waves 'rolling and gambolling and slapping the rocks as if they were wild creatures who were perfectly free and tossed and tumbled and sported like this for ever' (p. 317).

The exhilaration of the waves has its counterpart in the lines running up and across in Lily's picture, with its greens and blues, and its attempt at something. In the sudden intensity of her vision, Lily draws her line and the form emerges. One would be very much surprised indeed if the relation of masses, lights and shadows in the picture did not portray the rising and falling of the waves, which echoes throughout the novel. . . .

From 'Some Aspects of Virginia Woolf's Imagery', *English Studies*, Vol. 41, 1960, pp. 180–96 (192–4).

VICTORIA SACKVILLE-WEST

Virginia Woolf and *Orlando*

I think it was made fairly clear in the recently published extracts from Virginia Woolf's diary that the idea of her book *Orlando* was inspired by her own strange conception of myself, my family, and Knole my family home. Such things as old families and great houses held a sort of Proustian fascination for her. Not only did she romanticize them—for she was at heart a born romantic—but they satisfied her acute sense of the continuity of history, English history in particular. These facts having been made clear for all to read in the printed pages of her diary, there can be no reason why I should not now reveal something of the inception of that book and its progress throughout the months she spent writing it, as related in various letters I received from her during that period.

The first letter is dated October 9, 1927, and it startled me considerably:

> Yesterday morning I was in despair. You know that bloody book which Dadie and Leonard extort, drop by drop from my breast? Fiction, or some title to that effect. I couldn't screw a word from me; and at last dropped my head in my hands, dipped my pen in the ink, and wrote these words, as if automatically, on a clean sheet: *Orlando, a Biography*. No sooner had I done this than my body was flooded with rapture and my brain with ideas. I wrote rapidly till twelve. Then I did an hour to fiction. So every morning I am going to write fiction (my own fiction) till twelve; and the other fiction till one. But listen: suppose Orlando turns out to be Vita, and its all about you and the lure of your mind—heart you have none—suppose there's the kind of shimmer of reality which sometimes attaches to my people as the lustre on an oyster shell—suppose, I say, that next October someone says 'There's Virginia gone and written a book about Vita', shall I mind? Say yes or no. Your excellence as a subject arises largely from your noble birth—but what's 400 years of nobility, all the same?—and the opportunity thus given for florid descriptive passages in great abundance. Though, I admit, I should like to untwine and twist again some very odd incongruous strands in you; and also, as I told you, it sprung upon me how I could revolutionize biography in a night; and so, if agreeable to you, I would like to toss this up in the air and see what happens. Yet, of course, I may not write another line.

You will come on Wednesday? You will write now, this instant, a nice humble letter of duty and devotion to me.

I am reading *Knole and the Sackvilles*. Dear me, you have a rich dusky attic of a mind. Oh yes, I want very much to see you.

I was not misled by this sudden, urgent desire for my company. I realized that it was the author's form of cupboard love—in other words, I had become 'copy'.

As we now know, she did write another line; many thousands of other lines: I think she really enjoyed writing this book and that it cost her less agony than many of the others. It represented her high spirits, her sense of humour, her sense of sheer fun, none of which are perhaps very apparent in the extracts we have been given from her diary. She was excited. Letters poured in. The next one begins, four days later:

'Well, thank God, Vita ain't coming,' I said, putting the telegram down with a snort. Why, asked Leonard, looking up from his handkerchief. To which I had no answer ready, but the true one came: Because my nose is red.

The poor Wolves have been having colds in the head....

... I am writing at great speed. For the third time I begin a sentence, the truth is ... The truth is I'm so engulfed in Orlando I can think of nothing else. It has ousted fiction, psychology, and the rest of that odious book completely. Tomorrow I begin the chapter which describes you and Sasha meeting on the ice. I am swarming with ideas.... Look here, I must come down and see you, if only to choose some pictures. I want one of a young Sackville, (male) temp. James 1st; another of a young Sackville, (female) temp. George III. Please lend yourself to my little scheme. It will be a little book, about 30,000 words at most, and at my present rate which is feverish (I think of nothing but you all day long in different guises) I shall have it done by Christmas. . . .

From 'Virginia Woolf and *Orlando*', *The Listener*, Vol. 53, January 27, 1955, pp. 157–8 (157).

JOHN GRAHAM

Parody in *Orlando*

... The subtitle of this book—*A Biography*—indicates the object of its most sustained parody. Virginia Woolf's life-long fondness for reading biographies, which she frequently reviewed for periodicals, must have led her on many a weary trek through tomes more remarkable for their pretentious style and solemn pedantry than for any real insight into the lives with which they dealt. From the stereotyped flourishes of the preface to the learned uselessness of its scholarly index, *Orlando* parodies this type of biography. But the ridicule goes farther than that. The absurdities of the biographer are the absurdities of the whole approach to things which she considered typically masculine: the pompous self-importance; the childish faith in facts, dates, documents, and 'evidence'; the reduction of truth to the logical conclusions deducible from such evidence; and the reluctance to deal with such nebulous aspects of life as passion, dream, and imagination. For all his learning and labour, the biographer does not understand his subject, and when understanding Orlando's life began to engross Virginia Woolf's serious attention, he became an encumbrance instead of a joke and disappeared from the book.

The parody of the biographer is most emphatic in those passages where he pauses solemnly to explain the obvious, to record with meticulous precision a trivial detail, to shake his head over the shocking state of the documents, to lament the paucity of facts, or to confess his dismay at having to deal with matters which decorum would suppress but which the dedicated scholar must record. Between these direct intrusions, the parody is sustained by the style; and here Virginia Woolf brilliantly solved a difficult technical problem. The biographer is a bore; we must know from the way he writes that he is a bore; but what he writes cannot bore us if we are to read 'his' book. The style nicely blends his pretensions to formal elegance with a driving narrative energy and a ready flow of exact and fresh imagery. The following passage illustrates this blend at its best, in the chapters dealing with the Elizabethans. Orlando is waiting for Sasha to join him:

> *Many a time* did Orlando, pacing the little courtyard, *hold his heart* at the sound of some *nag's* steady footfall on the cobbles, or at the rustle of a woman's dress. But the traveller was only some merchant, making home *belated;* or some woman of the quarter whose errand

was *nothing so innocent*. They passed, and the street was quieter than before. (1) Then those lights which burnt downstairs in the small, huddled quarters where the poor of the city lived moved up to the sleeping-rooms, and then, one by one, were *extinguished*. The street lanterns in these *purlieus* were few at most; and the *negligence* of the night watchman often *suffered them to expire* long before dawn. The darkness then became even deeper than before. (2) Orlando *looked to* the wicks of his lantern, saw to the saddle girths; primed his pistols; examined his holsters; and did all these things a dozen times at least till he could find nothing more needing his attention. (3) Though it still lacked some twenty minutes to midnight, he could not bring himself to go indoors to the inn parlour, where the hostess was still serving sack and the cheaper sort of Canary wine to a few seafaring men, who would sit there trolling their ditties, and telling their stories of Drake, Hawkins, and Grenville, till they toppled off the benches and rolled asleep on the sanded floor. The darkness was *more compassionate to his swollen and violent heart*. He listened to every footfall; *speculated on* every sound. Each drunken shout and each wail from some *poor wretch* laid in the straw or in other distress *cut his heart to the quick,* as if it *boded ill omen* to his *venture* (pp. 55–6).

The italicized words and phrases are removed slightly from current good usage (though not sufficiently to confuse their meaning), and sustain our sense of a style both consciously formal and 'elegant'. This is done by mixing genuinely archaic turns of phrase with modern clichés. Among the former are: *hold his heart, belated* (in the sense of 'made late'), *nothing so* innocent, suffered them *to* (with reference to an inanimate object like 'lights'), looked *to,* compassionate *to* (in the sense of 'showing compassion towards'), and speculated *on* (of a sensation, such as 'sound'). Formal diction, deriving from late eighteenth-century or early nineteenth-century prose style, is apparent in: *extinguished* (of lights), *purlieus, negligence, expire,* and *venture,* none of which is archaic. At the end of the paragraph, the stiffness of these 'refined' expressions modulates into the grosser absurdity of phrases which originated in romantic prose fiction and which are still clichés of the pulp romance: *many a time, his swollen and violent heart, some poor wretch, cut his heart to the quick, boded ill omen.* None of these requires any knowledge of specific works parodied, and none obtrudes so violently that amusement disrupts the momentum of the narrative.

The vigour and directness of the numbered sentences counterbalance this inflated manner: the visual image of the lights going out in the quarters of the poor, the kinetic swiftness of Orlando's fidgeting as he waits, and the image of the sailors telling stories and getting drunk are all simple and vivid. Such words as 'toppled' and 'rolled' offset with their energy the soggy clichés of the sentences which follow them; and even in these sentences, phrases like 'drunken shout . . . wail . . . laid in the straw' bolster up the slack words in which they are set. We are gently reminded of the biographer's stuffiness even as we enjoy the speed and energy of his narrative, which save his prose from becoming so tedious that it is unreadable.

When parody operates throughout an entire work in the manner of this passage, it ceases to be an added grace of wit and becomes, as in *Don Quixote*, a technique of presentation.[1] Assimilating as it may the extremes of satiric mockery and affectionate mimicry, this technique is elastic, permitting divergent feelings and attitudes to intertwine in such a way that they 'act creatively on each other, establishing new syntheses of feeling and stimulating more comprehensive and subtle perception'.[2] It allows conflicting elements to marry freely and to breed oppositions which lead not to the baffled sense of logical contradiction engendered by a related form, paradox, but to a comic recognition of the teeming illogicality of life. Sharply defined parodies are rare in *Orlando*: the intrusions of the biographer, where he self-consciously moralizes; some passages ridiculing Virginia Woolf's lyric style; the mental sonneteering of Orlando as he thinks of Sasha, or his Jacobean meditations on death; Lieutenant Brigge's diary, the pompous testament of The Briton Abroad; the sentimental letter of Miss Penelope Hartopp, the gushing flirt; the elaborate parody of the masque, when Modesty, Chastity, and Purity rant and posture around the bed of the transformed Orlando; the snippets of Victorian Female Verse—these, and a few other short passages, strike our *conscious* attention as parodies. Without the enveloping parody of the biographer's style, they would be too sudden and brief to be effective; with it, they affect us as quick rays of wit flashing out from an ambience more diffuse than they but identical in kind.

The mocking gleam of parody is shed also by the clouds of allusion which float lightly over most of the narrative in the first four chapters. Consider, for example, the opening scene of the book, the charm of which is founded on the universal adult reaction to youthful ardour, a reaction which can range from approving indulgence to ironic sadness, depending on the control of tone. In this case, a comic tone is sustained by defining Orlando's ardour through a parody of romance, which first appears in the last sentence of the first paragraph: 'Orlando's father, or perhaps his grandfather, had struck it from the shoulders of a vast Pagan who had started up under the moon in the barbarian fields of Africa; and now it swung, gently, perpetually, in the breeze which never ceased blowing through the attic rooms of

---

[1] I am indebted in the following discussion to Dorothy Van Ghent's comments on parody in her book, *The English Novel, Form and Function*, New York, 1953, pp. 11-18.

[2] *Ibid.*, p. 13.

the gigantic house of the lord who had slain him.' The uncertainty about which ancestor won this trophy is balanced by the grandiose emphasis of *vast Pagan,* which is echoed by *gigantic house* at the end of the sentence; and between these two portentious phrases the crude elements of romance are tossed before us in the picture of the Pagan *starting up under the moon in the barbarian fields of*—not Yorkshire, by any means, but the inevitably exotic Africa. In the opening sentence of the second paragraph, the allusive note is maintained: 'Orlando's fathers had ridden in fields of *asphodel,* and stony fields, and fields watered by *strange* rivers . . .'; but this is balanced anticlimatically by 'and they had struck *many* heads of *many* colours off *many* shoulders', which reduces their heroic exertions to a kind of vague trophy collecting, very much as if they had absent-mindedly been gathering a splendid array of the footballs which this particular head resembled. Then we are confronted by the grave youth who moves in the mental world which has just been parodied: 'So too would Orlando, he vowed.' The affectionate mockery generated by this scene carries over into the whole section devoted to the Elizabethans and Jacobeans, where the parodistic treatment of courtly love, the courtier's life, and melancholy obsessions with Death, Fame, and the *vita brevis* are in effect a tribute to the abdundant belief of an age in which men pursued values from which, for better or worse, we are detached. . . .

From 'The "Caricature Value" of Parody and Fantasy in *Orlando*', *University of Toronto Quarterly,* Vol. 30, 1961, pp. 345–66 (353–6).

JEAN GUIGUET

The Waves

... Hitherto, for lack of a better term, I have used the word 'monologue' or 'voice' to describe what the characters say; I must point out, however, that neither of these words is satisfactory. These are not voices, in the sense that they are not differentiated. But for the 'Bernard said' or 'Jinny said' that introduces them, they would be indistinguishable; they have the same texture, the same substance, the same tone. Only apparently has a herald replaced the narrator; it would be truer to say that the poet has replaced the characters. Thus we come to that other aspect of *The Waves*, the poem, and a study of this will enable us to define not only the language, but the true nature of these so-called monologues.

Each time she attempted to picture clearly to herself the still uncertain aspect of her new book, Virginia Woolf invariably mentioned its poetic character. Yet since she speaks of her previous novels as 'these serious poetic experimental books...'[1] the adjective by itself tells us little. We must seek other references: 'Away from facts' (p. 104); 'the idea of some continuous stream' (p. 108); 'Something abstract poetic...' (p. 128); 'an abstract mystical eyeless book....' (p. 137). If we remember what Virginia Woolf means by abstract, not only do we realize that there is no contradiction between abstraction and poetry, but we begin to see in what sense the latter term must be understood; and at the same time the substance, as well as the form, of *The Waves* becomes clearer. The word 'mystic', moreover, leads us in the same direction, implying a direct contact between sensibility and intelligence fused in a single act, that of apprehending a truth and a reality which eludes our ordinary awareness. And when Virginia Woolf contrasts this mystical aspiration with what words give us— 'what I say, what people say' (p. 137)—we realize that the verb *say* ('he said, she said') introducing each speaker in *The Waves* does not bear its ordinary meaning, that the voice it refers to speaks through no mouth, has no individual timbre, does not use the language of everyday. And to define that voice is to solve the whole problem of *The Waves*—for the reader, as it was for the author.

On one of her various attempts to get started, Virginia Woolf writes: '... several problems cry out at once to be solved. Who thinks it? And am I outside the thinker? One wants some device which is not a trick'

[1] *A Writer's Diary*, p. 105.

(p. 146). This thinker is to become Bernard, Neville or Susan—but not entirely, since they are not detached from one another as their separate names and bodies and apparent destinies might suggest. And this effacement of their individuality, of the differences between them, only increases the temptation, for the author to mingle with them, to become part of them. Already, faced with the same problem, she has let slip the word 'autobiography' (p. 143); which indicates that these are not six voices in search of characters, but a single being in search of voices. Moreover, these voices, originally merged in one single voice—the thinker, She—as, basically, they still remain, behind the literary convention which has divided them, ought to be anonymous: 'I don't want a Lavinia or a Penelope; I want "she" ' (p. 143). It might almost be said that the problem comes down to 'placing' these voices, almost in the physical sense of the expression, so that while preserving a certain individuality, while remaining faithful to the basic differences from which they emanate and which their purpose is to express, they do not rise above the submerged level at which they communicate in an undifferentiated tone and where they are as yet uncontaminated by the surface of things, of people, of life. To define this position and to hold it, that was the vital task: 'I am convinced that I am right to seek for a station whence I can set my people against time and the sea—but Lord, the difficulty of digging oneself in there, with conviction' (p. 149). This region is not governed by those conjunctions of space and time which give solidity to thought and being; it lies at a level of consciousness which may justify the use of the term 'interior monologue'. But it should be clearly understood that this interior monologue has nothing in common with what the term usually implies—the verbal transcription of the stream of consciousness, to a greater or lesser depth according to each author.

At this point, poetry has to be brought in. What we find in *The Waves* is neither the transcription nor even the translation into words of the inner life at the conscious or subconscious level defined above, but what might be called, borrowing a formula from T. S. Eliot, its poetic correlative. By this I mean a way of writing, a style, which is essentially that of the writer, freed from any preoccupation with realism, calling on all his resources, knowledge and skill with words to obtain an equivalent to the sort of reality he is trying to express. What Bernard, Rhoda, Louis, etc. 'say' is just, in fact, what they do not say, it is not even what they think or what they feel, whether clearly or confusedly, but what will affect the reader's sensitivity and intelligence so as to make him conceive and feel, as though by direct experience, the conscious or subconscious reality which might form the stuff of their true interior monologue, in the usual sense of the term. Bernard, in his final summing-up, considers his own mental attitude, and incidentally provides a definition: '... that which is beyond and outside our own predicament; to that which is symbolic, and thus perhaps permanent, if there is any permanence in our sleeping, eating, breathing, so animal, so spiritual and tumultuous lives' (p. 176).

Simultaneously, this interpretation sheds light on the epithet 'mystical' which Virginia Woolf often uses about this book. It refers to that direct access to 'reality', to what is true and essential, which is the result of poetry. And this invalidates all criticism of these monologues, made from the point of view of realism, on the grounds of their generalized character, their lack of verisimilitude—which is particularly striking in the early pages, where the speakers are children—or of the monotony of these voices, distinguished by no individual accent.

If the formal characteristics of *The Waves* seem thus, on the one hand, to correspond to the author's intentions and, on the other, to be justified by their logical consistency, this may be attributed to the author's mastery and virtuosity; but it is only by examining the reality which has been cast in this form and which is revealed by it that we can judge whether the form itself came from a compelling need, or was merely a display of technical skill.

We can readily recognize in *The Waves* that favourite subject of Virginia Woolf's: the unity and multiplicity of personality, in its relations with the outside world of things and other people. The originality of this work, the undoubted advance shown over its predecessors, are due to the total elimination of elements alien to that 'reality' which the author is seeking to express:

> ... what I want now to do is to saturate every atom. I mean to eliminate all waste, deadness, superfluity: to give the moment whole; whatever it includes. Say that the moment is a combination of thought; sensation; the voice of the sea. Waste, deadness, come from the inclusion of things that don't belong to the moment; this appalling narrative business of the realist: getting on from lunch to dinner: it is false, unreal, merely conventional (p. 139).

This statement, made on November 28, 1928, while the novelist was still only at the groping, exploratory stage, sums up fairly well what she wants to eliminate and what she is seeking to convey. The sparse landmarks defining certain events in space and time, and those events themselves, which, from *Jacob's Room* to *To the Lighthouse,* had served as support, as scaffolding, and also as boundaries, to that transparent, fluid, shifting edifice in which Virginia Woolf tries to seize the essence of the inner life, these have disappeared.

Places have no longer any reality, even the sketchiest reality, outside the consciousness of the individuals, who both create them and assimilate their substance in a single act of perception. The house, the garden, the school, Louis' office, Jinny's room, Susan's farm, the restaurant at Hampton Court, are at no point, by no word, integrated into spatial reality or even co-ordinated with space. They do not exist

in space; no path leads to them, no map could reproduce their topo-
graphy; they exist only in relation to the consciousness on which the
novelist-poet concentrates exclusively. Time, too, is abolished. If it
seems to have slipped in furtively in the hour of a rendezvous, between
the pages of a calendar, compressed in a reference to someone's age,
it is as if by accident, like some frontier incident occurring at the
extreme limits between time and duration, when the mind loosens its
hold on the moment and seeks to get its bearings from that remote,
external line on which the minutes are marked out uniformly. But in
fact we must beware of the traps laid by the ambiguity of language.
Most frequently such expressions as 'eight o'clock', 'May or June',
'twenty-five years', even if the reader deduces therefrom an implicit
chronology, are charged with an emotional content which denatures
them and reintegrates them into the world of consciousness from which
they seem to have been detached. This is not part of a day or a year or
a human life; it is the point at which emotions converge—the eagerness
of friends about to meet, a longing for the countryside or for freedom,
a whole part of one's life compressed in a figure so as to be grasped in
its entirety. In the same way, the fleeting references to points in space,
such as London or Hampton Court, are no more part of ordinary
space than is the imaginary Elvedon. This is not the London, or the
Hampton Court, that may be as familiar to us as it is to the characters
in the book, but one which exists only in the mind that is aware of it
and which is really only a single bundle of sensations, images and
thoughts, hastily tied up and labelled.

Events, the material of a story, have disappeared also. They were
still to be found, however sparsely, in the earlier novels where, despite
their simplicity and ordinariness, they seemed to be connected with
the characters. Here there are only events of such a general nature—
school, university, profession, town life, country life, marriage or
celibacy, that they no longer count as incidents or accidents, as things
that happen. They melt into the texture of the whole of life. What we
are given is only the cluster of impressions on which the psyche has
fed; all that has remained external to it, all that might constitute
an event, strictly speaking, is eliminated.

What is left, then, for these voices to utter, if time no longer
exists to give order to their speech, if space no longer exists to contain
them and the things around them, to separate or bring them together,
if events no longer exist to form a story or stories in which they might
play their part and become characters?

'The Waves' is a poetic title, charged with complex potency as
well as with a multiplicity of meanings, and is thus mysterious. It
stresses the continuity—and also the eternity—of the discontinuous;
the conflict between time and duration, parallel to that between the
transitory and the permanent; it evokes cosmic forces that submerge
the frail voices of mankind, and intermittences that echo those of the

human heart. The eternal tide of reality, moving forward from the remote horizon to beat and break on the shores of consciousness, the deep unity underlying apparent plurality, these and a thousand other things are suggested in turn by the waves at each of their appearances in the novel. An equally characteristic, though less fascinating, title would have been 'Here and Now', which Virginia Woolf at one time considered giving to the book that became *The Years*. The fact that she says in her diary '*The Waves* is also here and now' (p. 215) may entitle us to read a valuable hint into this variant. Moreover, apart from this statement, which is an afterthought, we can refer to the recurrence of the phrase in the book itself (pp. 90, 100, 121, 159, 214).

It is the here-and-now, or (to use an equivalent and neater expression of Virginia Woolf's) the moment, that this play-poem, in my opinion, explores and strives to express. I have already noted the importance of 'the moment' for Virginia Woolf, in her life as well as in her work. I have stressed the capital importance of this experience, which is the centre of her psychological and intellectual life, and moreover the point on which all her work is focused. *The Waves*, after the not unrelated interlude of *Orlando*, marks her return to this fundamental preoccupation. Its originality and its value are due to the fact that it springs solely from this source, and that it exploits in a coherent manner all the data and all the consequences of that inner adventure which hitherto had provided only the culminating points, or indeed the starting-points, for her novels.

Before seeking a fuller definition in *The Waves* itself, we may turn to the sketch *The Moment: Summer's Night*[2] in which certain phrases formulate in brief abstract fashion the essential lines of the complex whole we are striving to grasp: '. . . everybody believes that the present is something, seeks out the different elements in this situation in order to compose the truth of it, the whole of it.' This is the postulate that must be accepted before venturing on *The Waves*, and without which the book has no meaning. 'To begin with: it [the present moment] is largely composed of visual and of sense impressions.' The words 'I see', 'I hear', 'Look', in the opening lines of *The Waves* fling pure sensations at the reader; but more than this, they are incantatory formulae which awaken his sensibility to the world of impressions into which he is entering. True, we immediately recognize the 'myriad impressions' received by the mind 'from all sides . . . an incessant shower of innumerable atoms' which, as early as 1919 [in 'Modern Fiction'] Virginia Woolf had declared it the novelist's task to convey

[2] Published for the first time in *The Moment and Other Essays*. It is interesting to note that Leonard Woolf's preface tells us that this was the first draft, a typescript copiously corrected by hand. Although no precise data entitle one to make the assumption, considering the affinities between this sketch and *The Waves* it is tempting to suppose that they date from the same period, and even that this is one of those little "sketches" that she wrote every morning "to amuse" herself while brooding over her novel. (*Diary*, p. 142)

'with as little mixture of the alien and external as possible'. But this was the first time she was going to follow literally, in a novel, her own critical suggestion and to concentrate unremittingly and uncompromisingly on rendering life as she had conceived it: 'a luminous halo, a semi-transparent envelope surrounding us from the beginning of consciousness to the end'. Moreover, the 1919 formulation is a general one; it expresses an intuition without, however, analysing it. The phrases are often quoted, on account of their concentration and their startling newness at the time. But they are only a point of departure; I have quoted them in order to stress the unity of Virginia Woolf's thought. We must return to *The Moment* to follow that thought to the final stages of its development.

'But this moment is also composed of a sense that the legs of the chair are sinking through the centre of the earth, passing through the rich garden earth; they sink, weighted down.' Sense impressions were the surface of the moment; here we have its depth, its relation with the rest of the universe, its roots in the darkness. That rich garden soil, that centre of the earth with which the moment brings us into contact, are all those forms of reality which, through the different layers of the concrete, lead us to the heart and essence of things. And our participation in this essence, our rootedness, is fate itself weighing us down.

Finally, the moment includes a third component, of a different nature: 'Here in the centre is a knot of consciousness; a nucleus divided up into four heads, eight legs, eight arms, and four separate bodies.' The other elements, whether peripheral or central, were detached and, so to speak, unsupported; they made up the multiplicity, the heterogeneity, the discontinuity of the moment. Perhaps this is the world of *Jacob's Room*, circumscribing a void in which something could be sensed, something had to be postulated: that something was the third element of the moment, this integrating power, this nucleus of consciousness. It may seem surprising that Virginia Woolf took so long to make so simple a discovery. But then its simplicity is only apparent. What is this consciousness? It is one and yet manifold; and it has always haunted Virginia Woolf. Remember that Septimus Smith was Clarissa Dalloway's 'double'; and the inextricable multiplicity of Orlando may be only an arabesque scribbled in the margin of the research that led up to *The Waves*. These separate consciousnesses, which, released from the prison of single bodies to which centuries of rationalist and pragmatic thought had confined them, are fused in the moment, are to be the central element in *The Waves*. And inversely, the succession of moments that makes up the book organize themselves around these consciousnesses, while merging with them to become their very substance. That dateless morning in the garden of their childhood means for each of the six protagonists what he is *for* and *through* the other five, as well as what he is *for* and *through* himself.

On this first layer all later experience will settle; their shared years at school, their meetings in youth and in maturity. And even in the inevitable separation imposed upon them by their individual destinies, the six consciousnesses will constantly adhere to one another. If each of them becomes a centre: Susan on her farm, Rhoda in her solitude, Jinny in her sensual adventures, Neville amongst his books, Louis at his office and Bernard in his social life, one or other of the rest is constantly appearing as though to ensure a relief or to make a contribution.

Naturally, this synthesis attains perfection on the two occasions when the six friends meet. On the first, when they are saying goodbye to Percival, the latter—a mythical figure through his silence, a symbol through his name—becomes the kingpin of this multiple consciousness. The others' love for him is the catalytic agent that gives rise to this perfect moment, 'the thing we have made, that globes itself here . . .'. To tell the content of 'this globe whose walls are made of Percival' (p. 104) one would have to quote the whole page. The moment holds all human things, all space, the happiness of a secluded life, of ordinary life, of fields and seasons, of the future which is still to be created and which they will create. This richness justifies Bernard's phrase: 'The moment was all; the moment was enough' (p. 197).

Does Percival's death mean the disintegration of this multiple consciousness? Does it bring to an end the eager quest which, through him, they all pursued? The twenty-fifth year, his departure and his death are perhaps only one and the same event. To measure the extent of this catastrophe, listen to Bernard, who has a gift for words, some twenty years after, at their final gathering:

> It was different once. . . . Once we could break the current as we chose. How many telephone calls, how many post cards, are now needed to cut this hole through which we come together, united, at Hampton Court? How swift life runs from January to December! We are all swept on by the torrent of things grown so familiar that they cast no shade; we make no comparisons; think scarcely ever of I or of you; and in this unconsciousness attain the utmost freedom from friction and part the weeds that grow over the mouths of sunken channels (p. 153).

Once, that's to say in their youth, when Percival was alive and their communion was a living thing, their intermingled consciousnesses, made keen by mutual contact, could grasp the profound reality of the universe and of life. Each in his own way and according to his individual tendencies, but stimulated and enriched by the differences between them, they went from one moment to the next, and each moment was fullness and knowledge and shared rebirth. The here-and-now, which was a miracle, has become a routine: it has been consciousness, voice and communion; it has become unconsciousness, silence and solitude. . . .

From Chapter 5 of *Virginia Woolf and Her Works*, The Hogarth Press, London, 1965, pp. 283–92. Some footnotes have been omitted.

JOSEPHINE O'BRIEN SCHAEFER

Percival's Role

...As Louis had foretold when he left school, life has divided them. In the fourth section, however, Virginia Woolf brings them together in a farewell party for Percival.[1] This episode best explains the appropriateness of the title *The Moths* which Virginia Woolf originally gave the novel. Percival never appears in his own person in *The Waves;* he is always being apprehended by one or other of the six characters, all of whom are attracted to him. Jinny and Bernard accept him as an attracting force: Susan is loved by him; Neville loves him. And even Louis who resents him and Rhoda who does not really come into full contact with him until after his death feel his power. All are bound together at this farewell party in a communal celebration of Percival, the man of action: the whole man, the simple man for whom being and doing are one. After Percival's death Bernard remembers him as sitting in the centre, a position he assumes for the reader during the party itself because of certain images introduced in the unspoken dialogue between Louis and Rhoda. Louis notes that the others 'have become nocturnal, rapt. Their eyes like moth's wings moving so quickly that they do not seem to move at all.' Rhoda adds that the guests seem to dance in a circle round a camp fire. Thus Percival has become the flame, the light around which their thoughts and emotions flicker like moths.

At this moment when 'the sun has bared its face', Rhoda, Louis, Neville, Susan, Jinny, and Bernard are no longer half-formed creatures. About to come into their own as adults, each circles about Percival for one moment, revealing the bright patch or the black mark which life has stamped upon him. Each remembers a specific moment from childhood and also heralds the world he is making for himself.

'Old Mrs Constable lifted her sponge and warmth poured over us,' said Bernard. 'We became clothed in this changing, this feeling garment of flesh.'

[1] William Tindall identifies Percival with Wagner's Parsifal (*The Literary Symbol*, p. 187). Leonard Woolf says Percival 'contains something of Thoby Stephen' ('Cambridge', *Sowing*, p. 136). Throughout the novel Percival is described as the simple man, the whole man, the man for whom action and self are one. His death, like Rachel's in *The Voyage Out*, makes him important. It underlines the frailty of human flesh and the haphazardness of events. As Bernard notes, 'What is startling, what is unexpected, what we cannot account for, what turns symmetry to nonsense – that comes suddenly to my mind, thinking of him' (p. 172).

'The boot-boy made love to the scullery-maid in the kitchen garden,' said Susan, 'among the blown-out washing.'

'The breath of the wind was like a tiger panting,' said Rhoda.

'The man lay livid with his throat cut in the gutter,' said Neville. 'And going upstairs I could not raise my foot against the immitigable apple tree with its silver leaves held stiff.'

'The leaf danced in the hedge without anyone to blow it,' said Jinny.

'In the sun-baked corner,' said Louis, 'the petals swam on depths of green' (p. 89).

Just as Bernard will always speak for the group, always use the *we*, Louis will stand, as he did in childhood, apart from the group in an enforced solitude. While Susan will have her natural happiness and escape the complicated world of man as man, Rhoda will fear this beast of a world which hunts her down, its breath at her heels. Neville's sense of death constricts the moment now and forever; but from Jinny the dancing leaf receives that awe, half fear and half admiration, due to life. At this moment of young adulthood when differences and not similarities are stressed, Virginia Woolf makes an exception of Louis and Rhoda. They alone are represented by memories other than their own particular motifs: the chained beast and the basin of petals. Soon to become lovers, they have exchanged motifs and affirm the area they have in common: Rhoda conveys the fear implicit in the chained beast, and Louis strikes the note of loneliness found in Rhoda's basin of white petals.

But with all their differences, the six characters form a unified circle. In celebrating their love for another, they create a pause and fill it with significance. Each one finds what he most persistently seeks in his own life suddenly made real in the communal feast. . . . Real and intense as the circle of illumination is, it lasts but a moment. The insistent demands of their individuality will break the circle and fling Bernard, Susan, Louis, Rhoda, Neville, and Jinny back into the turbulent waters of life.

For the moment, however, the annihilation of unity is withheld by the fact of Percival's death. Neville, Bernard, and Rhoda spin threads of communication as their emotions centre upon this fact. For Neville death is pain and loneliness: he remains fixed in the presence of 'the immitigable tree'. All men are doomed, he thinks: a carelessly adjusted strap can reduce anyone to ashes. Since the incoherence of life transfixes him, his own will to move is atrophied. Faced by Percival's death, Neville can only suffer: 'I sob, I sob.' Bernard, on the other hand, finds that he does not know which is sorrow, which joy; for Percival is dead and his own son is born. Death brings such loss and alteration to Bernard that he must be alone for a while to consider what has happened to his world. Bernard must recognize

G

the loss of his opposite: the man of simple emotions committed to action. Holding himself 'outside the machine', i.e. outside the usual order and sequence of his daily activities, Bernard tries to see by the light of Percival's death what is important in life. In this new perspective he sees death as a triumph, as the outfacing of the worst that the world can wreak on man. Rather than suffer as Neville does, Bernard attempts to contemplate. . . .

From Chapter 6 of *The Three-fold Nature of Reality in the Novels of Virginia Woolf*, Mouton and Co., The Hague, 1965, pp. 147–51. One footnote has been omitted.

BERNARD BLACKSTONE

Bernard's Summing-up

What is the meaning of it all? Bernard is the only speaker in the final section: he sums up, he tries to explain his own life, and by implication the lives of the others: 'the illusion is upon me that something adheres for a moment, has roundness, weight, depth, is completed'. But the illusion does not last. He sees that all his life he has been consoling himself with phrases and stories. Truth lies, perhaps, in tumult, in disintegration? He thinks of a stormy day, and its exhilaration. His mind goes back to the nursery, and a life made up of 'arrows of sensation'; with pity and love, and the determination to fight the brute forces of the world. 'We suffered terribly as we became separate bodies.' But Bernard is the artist standing apart; he is not hurt so easily. Over schooltime his memory wanders, over Cambridge and philosophy. It is all a flux, no pattern anywhere. Yet outside objects, like a willow-tree, seem to stand out of the flux and can thus be clung to.

I saw the figures beneath the beech-trees at Elvedon. The gardeners swept; the lady at the table sat writing. But I now made the contribution of maturity to childhood's intuitions—satiety and doom; the sense of what is unescapable in our lot; death; the knowledge of limitations; how life is more obdurate than one had thought it. Then, when I was a child, the presence of an enemy had asserted itself; the need for opposition had stung me. I had jumped up and cried, 'let's explore'. The horror of the situation was ended.

But now he knows there is nothing to end, nothing to explore. There is only noise and confusion. And only once has he known peace, 'a space cleared in the mind'. It was when, leaning over a gate, he found that his self had disappeared, lost—not, as the sages say, in a larger whole—but in nothingness, desertion.

The woods had vanished; the earth was a waste of shadow. No sound broke the silence of the wintry landscape. No cock crowed; no smoke rose, no train moved. A man without a self, I said. A heavy body leaning on a gate. A dead man. With dispassionate despair, with entire disillusionment, I surveyed the dust dance; my life, my friends' lives, and those fabulous presences, men with brooms, women writing, the willow-tree by the river—clouds and phantoms made of dust too, of dust that changed, as clouds lose and gain and take gold and red and lose their summits and billow this way and that, mutable, vain. I, carrying a notebook, making phrases, had recorded merely changes; a shadow, I had been sedulous to take note of shadows. How can I proceed now, I said, without a self, weightless and visionless, through a world weightless, without illusion?

This was the end, he had thought: this dereliction. But in reality he was undergoing an experience (may we call it purgation?) pre-paratory to the end: the shedding of the self. There is a vision beyond this vision. Suddenly, there comes the experience of moving about in 'the world seen without a self'. It is only when the self has been destroyed, indeed, that a new world can be seen. What he has been pursuing all these years, trying to piece glimpses of self-coloured illumination into a whole, is the wrong track. But now the lost land-scape returns.

So the landscape returned to me; so I saw fields rolling in waves of colour beneath me, but now with this difference; I saw but was not seen. I walked unshadowed; I came unheralded. From me had dropped the old cloak, the old response; the hollowed hand that beats back sounds. Thin as a ghost, leaving no trace where I trod, perceiving merely, I walked alone in a new world, never trodden; brushing new flowers, unable to speak save in a child's words of one syllable; without shelter from phrases—I who have made so many; unattended, I who have always gone with my kind; solitary, I who have always had someone to share the empty grate, or the cupboard with its hanging loop of gold. But how describe the world seen without a self? There are no words. Blue, red—even they distract, even they hide with thickness instead of letting the light through. How describe or say anything in articulate words again?—save that it fades, save that it undergoes a gradual transformation, becomes, even in the course of one short walk, habitual—this scene also. Blindness returns as one moves and one leaf repeats another. Loveliness returns as one looks, with all its train of phantom phrases. One breathes in and out substantial breath; down in the valley the train draws across the fields lop-eared with smoke.

But for a moment I had sat on the turf somewhere high above the flow of the sea and the sound of the woods, had seen the house, the garden, and the waves breaking. The old nurse who turns the pages of the picture-book had stopped and had said, 'Look. This is the truth.'

Yes, the vision is fleeting, passing 'even in the course of one short walk': but it is not, as the others were, partial. It is all-embracing and, while it lasts, all-satisfying. This is because the partial illumina-tions have been given up. They had been seen through the distorting medium of the self; the personality had got mixed up in them. But here the self is lost. Moreover, the nature of the true revelation is to be seen in its fruits, lasting beyond the revelation itself; and now Bernard tells us what these fruits are.

The first is indifference to what happens. 'It does not matter whom I meet. All this little affair of "being" is over.' The second is unconsciousness of where one is. 'Nor do I know exactly where we are. What city does that stretch of sky look down upon? Is it Paris, is it London where we sit, or some southern city of pink-washed houses lying under cypresses, under high mountains, where eagles soar? I do not at this moment feel certain.' The third is doubt about the reality of the material world. 'I begin now to forget; I begin to doubt the fixity of tables, the reality of here and now, to tap my knuckles smartly upon the edges of apparently solid objects and say, "Are you hard?" ' The fourth is the sense of identity with others. 'And now I ask, "Who am I?" I have been talking of Bernard, Neville, Jinny, Susan, Rhoda and Louis. Am I all of them? Am I one and distinct? I do not know. We sat here together. . . . This difference we make so much of, this identity we so feverishly cherish, was overcome.' The fifth fruit is the acceptance of every component of one's nature, even the most animal. 'There is the old brute, too, the savage, the hairy man who dabbles his fingers in ropes of entrails; and gobbles and belches; whose speech is guttural, visceral—well, he is here. . . . That man, the hairy, the ape-like, has contributed his part to my life.' The sixth fruit is an intense unselfish interest in things. 'When I look down from this transcendency, how beautiful are even the crumbled relics of bread! What shapely spirals the peelings of pears make—how thin, and mottled like some seabird's egg. Even the forks laid straight side by side appear lucid, logical, exact; and the horns of the rolls which we have left are glazed, yellow-plated, hard. I could worship my hand even, with its fan of bones laced by blue mysterious veins and ability to curl softly or suddenly crush—its infinite sensibility.' The seventh fruit is the loss of desires. 'Immeasurably receptive, holding everything, trembling with fullness, yet clear, contained—so my being seems, now that desire urges it no more out and away; now that curiosity no longer dyes it a thousand colours. It lies deep, tideless, immune, now that he is dead, the man I called Bernard. . . .' The eighth fruit is the feeling of omniscience. 'Let a woman come, let a young man in evening dress with a moustache sit down; is there anything that they can tell me? No! I know all that, too. . . . The shock of the falling wave which has sounded all my life, which woke me so that I saw the gold loop on the cupboard, no longer makes quiver what I hold.'

The moment of vision is transitory; these resultant moments of peace, with whatever they may owe to the fine old brandy and the quails, can be broken by a face coming in at the door. But they come together again, in silence, in solitude. Once the self has been lost, the secret is found. It is with a song of glory that the book ends.

Let me now raise my song of glory. Heaven be praised for solitude. Let me be alone. Let me cast and throw away this veil of being, this cloud that changes with the least breath, night and day, and all night and all day. While I sat here I have been changing. I have watched the sky change. I have seen clouds cover the stars, then free the stars, then cover the stars again. Now I look at their changing no more. Now no one sees me and I change no more. Heaven be praised for solitude that has removed the pressure of the eye, the solicitation of the body, and all need of lies and phrases.

Only one desire remains to break this calm: the desire to conquer Death. And thus the book ends.

Death is the enemy. It is death against whom I ride with my spear couched, and my hair flying back like a young man's, like Percival's, when he galloped in India. I strike spurs into my horse. Against you I will fling myself unvanquished and unyielding, O Death!

From Chapter 10 of *Virginia Woolf: A Commentary*, The Hogarth Press, London, 1949, pp. 177–81.

The Affirmation of *The Years*

... 'I do not want to go back into my past, [Eleanor] was thinking. I want the present.' This is [a] major idea: that the passage of time is anything but a tragedy; that human nature is in the process of becoming less imperfect, becoming in a creative evolution during which evil will be overcome and good triumph. This is the affirmation of the novel as a whole. Peggy mistakenly thinks that the past 'was so interesting; so safe; so unreal—that past of the 'eighties; and to her, so beautiful in its unreality'. But Eleanor, who has lived in that past, come through its goods and its bads, realizes that not the past but the future is safe and interesting, and that she must therefore live in the present. At the conclusion of the novel, during which Eleanor—somewhat like Bernard—has been moving toward a complete awareness, she has a final apprehension of meaning. Delia's party is breaking up; it is very late, almost dawn. Eleanor has been worrying about people's seeming inability to communicate: 'She held her hands hollowed; she felt that she wanted to enclose the present moment; to make it stay; to fill it fuller and fuller, with the past the present and the future, until it shone, whole, bright, deep with understanding.' At first she thinks this impossible.

It's useless, she thought, opening her hands. It must drop. It must fall. And then? she thought. For her too there would be the endless night; the endless dark. She looked ahead of her as though she saw opening in front of her a very long dark tunnel. But, thinking of the dark, something baffled her; in fact it was growing light. The blinds were white.

Here, so far, is a situation exactly like that at the conclusion of *The Waves*. But *The Years* is not content to end here, with only an abstract statement; it goes on. The caretaker's two little children enter (Delia wishes to give them cake) and sing a song: 'Etho passo tanno hair,/Fai donk to tu do,' and so on. No one can understand a word of what they are singing: 'It was so shrill, so discordant, and so meaningless.' But Eleanor, looking for a word that will describe this song—this strange, new language of the youngest generation—decides upon 'beautiful'. Then in the dawn Eleanor goes to the window. A cab stops in front of a house two doors down.

She was watching the cab. A young man had got out; he paid the driver. Then a girl in a tweed travelling suit followed him. He fitted his latch-key to the door. 'There,' Eleanor murmured, as he opened the door and they stood for a moment on the threshold. 'There!' she repeated as the door shut with a little thud behind them.

Then she turned round into the room. 'And now?' she said ... 'And now?' she asked, holding out her hands to [Morris].

With an empathy like Clarissa's—an empathy that enabled her to 'become' Martin in India—Eleanor looks at the newly married couple and grasps all the immense significance of their beginning: the pattern of a continual becoming toward right and good. She has been correct in her belief that 'there must be another life.... Not in dreams; but here and now, in this room, with living people.... This is too short, too broken. We know nothing even about ourselves. We're only just beginning ... to understand, here and there.' *The Years* concludes, just as *The Waves* had done, with a separate final descriptive sentence: 'The sun had risen, and the sky above the houses wore an air of extraordinary beauty, simplicity and peace.' This formalization of the philosophical perspective by means of immediate social and individual circumstance makes *The Years* the most persuasive of Virginia Woolf's novels. The final cab episode is additionally effective because it contrasts with a similar scene at the beginning of the novel when Delia, who wants very much to marry, watches from the same window a hansom approach the Pargiter house. And she wonders:

Was it going to stop at their door or not? ... to her regret, the cab-man jerked his reins ... the cab stopped two doors lower down ... they watched a young man ... get out of the cab. He stretched up his hand to pay the driver....

The young man ran up the steps into the house; the door shut upon him and the cab drove away....

Dropping the blind, Delia turned, and coming back into the drawing-room, said suddenly:

'Oh, my God!'

Here is the idea of fulfilment and nonfulfilment; it appears very much as it had done in *The Waves*. Thus Eleanor, though she is a spinster, is fulfilled in her mental androgyny and empathy; on the other hand, Nicholas Pomjalovsky longs for a new world, and is constantly trying to make a speech in which he can articulate what he believes to be real. His inability to communicate, to surrender his identity, is symbolized—as was Neville's in *The Waves*—by his perversion. Sara Pargiter, perhaps the most pathetic person in the novel, is another example of nonfulfilment, although she herself is not entirely to blame for her inability to communicate. Extremely perceptive and sensitive, Sara is physically deformed; her behaviour becomes more and more erratic as she grows older, her fantastic manner being a shield between herself and the society that she feels hostile to her. She is reduced to poverty after her parents' sudden death, and lives with her sister Maggie in a shabby walk-up flat. Maggie—who resembles Susan of *The Waves,* though she is far more human and successful a character —marries, and Sara is left alone. For a time she turns to the Church of England; she finally falls in love, but with Nicholas, who, although he loves her very much, is quite candid in explaining why he cannot marry her. Sara's final rejection of society and social intercourse is symbolized by her arriving at Delia's party—after a dinner with North in her sordid boarding house, in what is perhaps the most superbly achieved sequence in the novel—wearing one blue stocking and one white.

Although society is the immediate background of individual behaviour in this novel, the use of society is not exactly conventional; it is not one social code, a single set of manners, that is emphasized, but rather the change from society to society—the social shift. As Virginia Woolf wrote in *The Waves,* 'Bodies, I note, already begin to look ordinary; but what is behind them differs—the perspective'. The very climax of the novel is Eleanor's dismissal of the faithful (and wonderful) Pargiter servant Crosby; together with Eleanor's sale of the Pargiter house, this constitutes her disposal of the last remnants of the old culture and tradition. This scene is filled with sadness and nostalgia; yet, although Eleanor weeps, 'she was so glad'. After this it is Crosby who preserves the old way, setting up pictures of the family in the little room where she boards, until 'it was quite like home'. For Eleanor it is not the seeming security of a traditional social context, but the apparently amorphous becoming of the future, that has value. Static society, then—as distinct from responsible human behaviour—is repudiated in *The Years* too as a superimposition. This is also made clear at Delia's final party, in a 'matter-spirit' contrast between Eleanor and her sister Milly. North looks at Milly and her husband Hugh—both of whom exist entirely as social creatures— and thinks, 'Tut-tut-tut, and chew-chew-chew—as they trod out the soft steamy straw in the stable; as they wallowed in the primeval swamp, prolific, profuse, half-conscious.' The damning word is of course 'half-conscious': Milly and Hugh have regressed, until in them, as in prehistoric life, awareness is choked with matter. For Eleanor —and it is toward Eleanor's point of view that North is gradually moving—life has not this static nature; it is 'a perpetual discovery'. . . .

From Chapter 5 of *The Glass Roof: Virginia Woolf as a Novelist,* University of California Press, Berkeley, 1954, pp. 137–41.

C. BASHAM

Between the Acts

... The overwhelming impression is of disintegration, and, as is always the case with Mrs Woolf's novels, the title offers a significant clue to this theme. It is typical of the complexity and comprehensiveness of this novel that the title should lend itself with equal force to several interpretations, each contributing to this central theme. It refers most obviously to the intervals in the village pageant when 'the audience slipped the noose, split up into scraps and fragments'; then to that longer interval between the first and second European wars; and the development of this latter theme makes it clear that it refers also to the strained relationship between Isa and Giles Oliver. So it is that the preparations for a performance of a village pageant, and the aftermath of the performance, assume a deeper significance. Yet the reader doesn't feel that the author is working outwards from her material as though it were representational or purely symbolic, so much as laying bare the significance of the surface reality itself, in the year 1939. She is not impressing a point of view upon the reader by means of symbol and imagery, as in *To the Lighthouse,* but is, rather, showing him what in retrospect he feels he might have noticed himself, had he been sufficiently aware.

Within the three themes to which the title relates, there is a complex tissue of events, sensations and thoughts which contribute to them. That which is most stressed is the frustration of Miss La Trobe, producer and author of the pageant, and there can be little doubt that Mrs Woolf is conscious, in portraying this character, of the artist, such as herself. As an instance of that change of tone between this and earlier novels it is interesting to contrast Miss La Trobe with an earlier artist, Lily Briscoe. In *To the Lighthouse* the latter completes her painting and has her vision; the former, when she attempts to create unity and realize her vision, is stricken with a sense of frustration:

> Now Miss La Trobe stepped from her hiding. Flowing and streaming, on the grass, on the gravel, still for one moment she held them together—the dispersing company. Hadn't she, for twenty-two minutes, made them see? A vision imparted was relief from agony ... for one moment ... one moment. Then the music petered out on the last word *we.* She heard the breeze rustle in the branches. She saw Giles Oliver with his back to the audience. Also Cobbet of

Cobbs Corner. She hadn't made them see. It was a failure, another damned failure! As usual. Her vision escaped her (p. 117).

And at the end of the pageant 'Dispersed are we, the gramophone informed them' (p. 230).

But not only are the audience dispersed: the main characters too are separated to an unusual degree. Isa, attracted to Rupert Haines, a gentleman farmer, suffers a breach from her husband (a stockbroker who had wished to be a farmer) and he from her, in his miserable and frustrated pursuit of Mrs Manresa, a visitor to Pointz Hall. Isa, too, is separated from her children, a relationship which is symbolically presented early in the novel:

> She tapped on the window with her embossed hairbrush. They were too far off to hear. The drone of the trees was in their ears; the chirp of birds; other incidents of garden life, inaudible, invisible to her in the bedroom, absorbed them (p. 20).

Old Bartholomew, lost in memories of India, destroys the world of the small child, his grandson, as he grubs among the flowers, and is adamantly unsympathetic towards his sister's avoidance of unpleasant truths and her 'one-making':

> 'What's the origin—the origin—of that?'
> 'Superstition,' he said.
> She flushed, and the little breath too was audible that she drew in as once more he struck a blow at her faith (p. 33).

Often in her novels Virginia Woolf conveys the thoughts of her characters when they are alone, meditating and remembering, but in this novel more than any of the others there is a feeling of loneliness and isolation as the characters meditate, as though a barrier is placed between them and others. Even Lucy Swithin and her brother are separated irremediably, in spite of their love for each other:

> But brother and sister, flesh and blood was not a barrier, but a mist. Nothing changed their affection, no argument, no fact; no truth. What she saw he didn't; what he saw she didn't—and so on, ad infinitum (p. 33).

This general state of isolation, or at least separation, is the more poignant because it is clear that the characters have a strong natural desire for contact with others: Miss La Trobe with her audience; Isa with her children; Bartholomew with his grandson; and Lucy Swithin not only with her brother, but with Miss La Trobe between the acts of the pageant:

> She gazed at Miss La Trobe with a cloudless old-aged stare. Their eyes met in a common effort to bring a common meaning to

birth. They failed; and Mrs Swithin, laying hold desperately of a fraction of her meaning, said: 'What a small part I've had to play! But you've made me feel I could have played . . . Cleopatra!' (p. 179).

One character who seems to epitomize this general sense of isolation is William Dodge, a visitor to Pointz Hall. He is separated from his kind in his homosexuality, and unable to make contact even with those who, like Lucy Swithin, seek to understand and help. During one of the intervals she shows him over Pointz Hall:

> And he wished to kneel before her, to kiss her hand, and to say: 'At school they held me under a bucket of dirty water, Mrs Swithin; when I looked up the world was dirty, Mrs Swithin; so I married, but my child's not my child, Mrs Swithin. I'm a half-man, Mrs Swithin; a flickering, mind-divided little snake in the grass, Mrs Swithin; as Giles saw; but you've healed me. . . .' So he wished to say; but said nothing; and the breeze went lolloping along the corridors, blowing the blinds out (p. 90).

It is interesting to contrast the unfortunate William Dodge with another homosexual, Nicholas, in *The Years,* as an indication of the difference in tone and outlook between the two novels. The latter enjoys complete personal and social ease.

The tragedy of this social malaise experienced by the characters in *Between the Acts* is that at a certain point a disintegration in personal relationships must inevitably lead to a disintegration of the person. This is most apparent in the case of William Dodge, but it is implicit also in Isa's infatuation for Rupert Haines, Giles's pursuit of Mrs Manresa, and Miss La Trobe's escape to the solace of the public house.

Behind and beyond the purely personal there are other forces at work, all contributing to the theme of disintegration. Just as Mrs Woolf lays bare the malaise of the most conventional, secure and well-established inhabitants of a conventional and secure country house, so she dissects the contemporary scene and strips it of all pretence. There is an interesting passage in *The Years* in which Mrs Woolf establishes her derision of Oxford by identifying the University with a tree which, three centuries ago, flourished, but now 'it was half fallen and had to be propped up by a stake in the middle' (p. 66). The same general method is adopted, but with greater skill, in *Between the Acts*. Contemporary life is reduced to pettiness and triviality by isolating certain significant aspects of it which, compared to earlier times, have become devalued. Isa Oliver enters the library at Pointz Hall:

> Then she added, stepping across the threshold: 'Books are the mirrors of the soul.'

In this case a tarnished, a spotted soul. For as the train took over three hours to reach this remote village in the very heart of England, no one ventured so long a journey, without staving off possible mind-hunger, without buying a book on a book-stall. Thus the mirror that reflected the soul sublime, reflected also the soul bored. Nobody could pretend, as they looked at the shuffle of shilling shockers that weekenders had dropped, that the looking-glass always reflected the anguish of a Queen or the heroism of King Harry (pp. 22–3).

And it becomes apparent a little later in the book, when Isa browses in the library, that just as the present is trivial, so the past which emerges into it has accordingly been reduced in stature. As a comment on the condition of the present, Isa, unable to find solace in 'The Antiquities of Durham: the Proceedings of the Archaeological Society of Nottingham', reads an account of a rape in a barrack-room at Whitehall, reported in *The Times*.

There are many instances, in this novel, of the deflation of the past. References to history and pre-history abound. The house, neighbourhood, and settled traditional life of the village make this kind of awareness possible without the suggestion that the author is introducing the theme of the past for its own sake. The past is organically part of the present of the novel. As part of the present it is trivial. There is the suggestion, throughout the novel, that the countless ages of man have led to *this* mis-shapen creature. This is the significance of its being Mrs Swithin who is the vehicle of thoughts of pre-history. She is certainly more sympathetically presented than Miss Kilman in *Mrs Dalloway*, but Mrs Woolf cannot allow her, with her vague religious feelings (rather than thoughts) and her self-appointed role as a unifier, to pass without censure. She has 'a ring on her finger and the usual trappings of rather shabby but gallant old age, which included in her case a cross gleaming gold on her breast' (p. 14). And there is a ludicrous incongruity in the fact of this old lady 'with a high nose and thin cheeks' awaiting morning tea in her bedroom and meditating on 'the iguanodon, the mammoth, and the mastodon'. This nullifying of the past by presenting it in the light of the present is a dominant theme. At the outset 'The old man in the arm-chair—Mr Oliver, of the Indian Civil Service, retired—said that the site they had chosen for the cesspool was, if he had heard aright, on the Roman road' (p. 8). The evocation of the past is far removed from that which, in an earlier novel, inspired Jacob Flanders. It is a past without stature, fit only for casual reference in light conversation and the idle reading of an old woman. The present has rendered the past insignificant.

The pageant substantiates this theme. Its aim—to represent the history of Britain from its creation to the present day—is geared towards installing electric light in the old church. The historical characters are interpreted by a set of country yokels:

The sound of horses' hooves, energetically represented by Albert the idiot with a wooden spoon on a tray, died away (p. 167).

A long line of villagers in shirts made of sacking began passing in and out in single file behind her between the trees.... They were singing, but not a word reached the audience (p. 95).

The theme of deflation is perhaps best summed up in the words of Lady Harpy Harraden in the Restoration scene: 'I that was Aurora Borealis am shrunk to a tar barrel. I that was Cassiopeia am turned to a she-ass' (p. 172).

It is the present, however, with which Mrs Woolf is concerned, and its stature is necessarily reduced by its contiguity with an insignificant past. This is the significance of the kaleidoscopic picture of past time dissolving into present time at the end of the pageant, when mirrors are flashed at the audience, who, glancing in embarrassment at their fragmentary reflections, hear a 'megaphonic, anonymous, loud-speaking' utterance:

I too have had some, what's called, education.... Look at ourselves, ladies and gentlemen! Then at the wall; and ask how's this wall, the great wall, which we call, perhaps miscall, civilization, to be built by (here the mirrors flickered and flashed) orts, scraps, and fragments like ourselves? (p. 219).

As though to bear witness to the truth of this utterance the audience, after the pageant, disintegrates into unsifted and incoherent disunity while the gramophone plays 'Dispersed are we':

'But you must remember,' the old cronies chatter, 'they had to do it on the cheap. You can't get people, at this time o' year, to rehearse. There's the hay, let alone the movies.... What we need is a centre. Something to bring us all together.... The Brookes have gone to Italy, in spite of everything. Rather rash? ... If the worst should come—let's hope it won't—they'd hire an aeroplane, so they said.... What amused me was old Streatfield, feeling for his pouch. I like a man to be natural, not always on a perch.... Then those voices from the bushes.... Oracles? You're referring to the Greeks? Were the oracles, if I'm not being irreverent, a foretaste of our own religion? Which is what? ... Crepe soles? That's so sensible.... They last much longer and protect the feet.... But I was saying: can the Christian faith adapt itself? In times like these.... At Larting no one goes to church.... There's the dogs, there's the pictures.... It's odd that science, so they tell me, is making things (so to speak) more spiritual.... The very latest notion, so I'm told, is, nothing's solid.... There, you can get a glimpse of the church through the trees ...' (pp. 231–2).

In this confused tangle of religion, science, and crepe soles there is the rumour of war. Giles is conscious of it throughout the novel, and thinks with anger of Europe 'bristling with guns, poised with planes. At any moment guns would rake that land into furrows; planes splinter Bolney Minster into smithereens and blast the Folly' (p. 66).

So much, then, for the past and present. The novel ends with the rise of the curtain on the future, but quite without the suggestion of hope found in *The Years*, or of the fulfilment which is experienced in *To the Lighthouse*. Rather, the present of 1939 is precariously balanced—or hemmed in—between a trivial past and an ominous future:

'The doom of sudden death hanging over us,' he said. 'There's no retreating and advancing'—he was thinking of the old lady show-ing him the house—'for us as for them.'
The future shadowed their present, like the sun coming through the many-veined transparent vine leaf; a criss-cross of lines making no pattern (p. 136).

Yet the present is not completely blank. There are still moments of cohesion and wholeness, though they are only moments. There is for example the illusion of the pageant which at moments is continued by the happy intrusion of nature: by the bellowing of the cows—'the primeval voice sounding in the ear of the present moment'; by the sudden downpour of rain which fell 'like all the people in the world weeping'; or by music:

Like quicksilver sliding, filings magnetized, the distracted united. The tune began; the first note meant a second; the second a third. Then down beneath a force was born in opposition; then another. On different levels they diverged.... Compelled from the ends of the horizon; recalled from the edge of appalling crevasses; they crashed; solved; united. And some relaxed their fingers; and others uncrossed their legs (pp. 220-1).

Recognition of the participation of producer, actors, audience and nature in the business of the pageant helps us to place the pageant itself in its perspective within the novel's total effect and meaning. Just as the past and the present are set off against each other while remaining part of the same continuous flow leading to the future, so the pageant too flows over into the life of the present, drawing sus-tenance from it and at the same time contributing to it. The vision of Miss La Trobe, for example, and her realization that it had 'escaped her', making the pageant, in spite of momentary success, 'another damned failure', is to have repercussions later in the novel, linking her with characters whom she has not met. After the 'triumph, humilia-tion, ecstasy, despair' of the pageant, when she is making her way to her house and the inn, she stops to look at the surrounding land and conceives another vision: ' "I should group them," she murmured, "here." It would be midnight; there would be two figures, half concealed by a rock. The curtain would rise. What would the first words be? The words escaped her' (p. 246). Later, in the public house, 'sitting arms akimbo with her glass before her' she returns to the same idea: 'There was the high ground at midnight; there the rock; and two scarcely perceptible figures. Suddenly the tree was pelted with starlings. She set down her glass. She heard the first words' (p. 248).

For the realization of Miss La Trobe's vision Mrs Woolf returns us, at the close of the book, to the family at Pointz Hall, where Giles and Isa are seen to be 'the two scarcely perceptible figures':

> The old people had gone up to bed. Giles crumpled the newspaper and turned out the light. Left alone together for the first time that day, they were silent. Alone, enmity was bared; also love. Before they slept, they must fight; after they had fought, they would embrace. From that embrace another life might be born. But first they must fight, as the dog fights with the vixen, in the heart of darkness, in the fields of night.
>
> Isa let her sewing drop. The great hooded chairs had become enormous. And Giles too. And Isa too against the window. The window was all sky without colour. The house had lost its shelter. It was night before roads were made, or houses. It was the night that dwellers in caves had watched from some high place among rocks.
>
> Then the curtain rose. They spoke (pp. 255–6).

This and the other quotations which have been offered are sufficient to show that the kind of reality which Virginia Woolf is attempting to convey in this novel demands much more than straightforward narrative. The material and language are so finely organized that by means of symbol, suggestion, and lyrical devices it can contain several layers of meaning. It is an inclusive prose which the author offers. Isa, with her fluent poetic fancy, is the main vehicle for such passages. The following extract with its illogicalities, inconclusiveness and symbolism is typical of Virginia Woolf's technique in *Between the Acts*: the lyrical and the narrative are immediately juxtaposed:

> 'This year, last year, next year, never....' Isa murmured. Her hand burnt in the sun on the window sill. Mrs Swithin took her knitting from the table.
>
> 'Did you feel,' she asked, 'what he said: we act different parts but are the same?'
>
> 'Yes,' Isa answered. 'No,' she added. It was Yes, No. Yes, yes, yes, the tide rushed out embracing. No, no, no, it contracted. The old boot appeared on the shingle.
>
> 'Orts, scraps, and fragments,' she quoted what she remembered of the vanishing play (p. 251).

There is no attempt in this novel at the method of direct stream-of-consciousness, for this would make it impossible for the author to convey those suggestions of which the character himself is not aware, which point, for the reader, to a wider significance. The stream-of-consciousness is inward-turning, revealing interior thoughts, or, as so often in Virginia Woolf's novels, the texture of thought rather than the thought itself. In *Between the Acts* however, the author is seeking comprehensiveness, and is therefore attempting to enclose wide ranges of meaning in this story of a small group of people in a country house setting on a single day in June. The result is a stylized, consciously lyrical stream-of-consciousness, as though the characters of *The Waves* were placed within a narrative context. In this way, without the author's intrusion, characters are presented at one and the same time as actors and chorus. The following quotation may help to illustrate this. Isa has wandered off, alone, into the gardens of Pointz Hall, during one of the intervals in the pageant. The passage, in addition to its narrative interest, reflects her present emotional state and the rift with her husband. More than this however, the lyricism of her thoughts reflects and underlines the tone of the whole novel: the sense of malaise in the present, the weight of an unhelpful past, and, as a result of these, the unpredictable hardships of the future. Desolation and isolation are the keynotes.

'Where do I wander?' she mused. 'Down what draughty tunnels? Where the eyeless wind blows? And there grows nothing for the eye. No rose. To issue where? In some harvestless dim field where no evening lets fall her mantle; nor sun rises. All's equal there. Unblowing, ungrowing are the roses there. Change is not; nor the mutable and lovable; nor greetings nor partings; nor furtive findings and feelings, where hand seeks hand and eye seeks shelter from eye.'

She had come into the stable yard where the dogs were chained; where the buckets stood; where the great pear tree spread its ladder of branches against the wall. The tree whose roots went beneath the flags, was weighted with hard green pears. Fingering one of them she murmured: 'How am I burdened with what they drew from the earth; memories; possessions. This is the burden that the past laid on me, last little donkey in the long caravanserai crossing the desert. "Kneel down" said the past. "Fill your pannier from our tree. Rise up, donkey. Go your way till your heels blister and your hoofs crack!" ' (pp. 181–2).

It is well known that Mrs Woolf was dissatisfied with this novel, which remains unrevised. Further, critics have suggested that the novel lacks 'completeness'—that nothing is resolved—and that it remains detached from life. These strictures seem to arise partly from the absence of clear resolution such as is found for example in *Mrs Dalloway* and *To the Lighthouse*. Yet the complex affinity between Miss

H

La Trobe and Giles and Isa at the close of the novel seems to me more satisfactory and acceptable as a contribution to the novel's meaning and structure than the completion of the design of Mrs Dalloway's experience as a result of the suicide of Septimus Warren Smith, or the return of Mrs Ramsay and the completion of Lily Briscoe's painting at the moment when Mr Ramsay and his children land at the lighthouse. It is true that *Between the Acts* does not lend itself to a summary interpretation of its meaning. The novel's complex symbolist lyricism does not lend itself to the precise definition of, for example, the colour symbolism of *To the Lighthouse* which, as Dr Daiches has shown, can be deduced almost by a process of mathematical equivalence, with blue and green standing for impersonality and so forth. But a novel which attempts to portray the spirit of an age, a period of time poised unhappily between a past which has lost its significance and a future whose only hope is that 'a new life might be born' can scarcely, if the author be honest to her vision, end on a note of resolution and fulfilment.

From '*Between the Acts*', *Durham University Journal*, Vol. 52, 1959, pp. 87–94 (88–93). Some footnotes have been omitted.

A. D. MOODY

The Maturity of *Between the Acts*

... [*Between the Acts*] is at least among her best three novels, along with *To the Lighthouse* and *The Waves;* and it is more mature than either of those. Certainly *To the Lighthouse* is the more highly wrought work of art: but when it is put beside *The Waves* and *Between the Acts*, the refinement of the art seems not to effect a more valuable grasp on experience, but rather to compensate for an ultimate unwillingness to accept the human condition. There is only the art itself, as it is represented in Lily Briscoe, to preserve the novel from the desolation threatened in its middle section. In *The Waves* Virginia Woolf had rejected the comforts of art's illusion, through Bernard and in the placing of Rhoda, and, accepting that the human condition is immitigably one of flux and process, had sought out and affirmed such positive powers as men have to control and construct their lives within nature. *Between the Acts* takes up the same concerns and significantly develops them.

For one thing it incorporates the historical dimension which in *The Waves* was barely noticed; so that instead of merely affirming the continuity of human life, it essays a critical scrutiny of the meaning and value of history for the present. Secondly, the function of the artistic imagination which was overstressed in *To the Lighthouse*, and deliberately played down in *The Waves*, is here established in a more justly balanced relationship with life. The artist, in this case Miss La Trobe, is not set like Lily Briscoe to cultivate an aesthetic sphere, outside and rather in opposition to the process and actuality of life; she is a mind merged in its process, as much as Bernard, but as a conscious and effectual artist, which he was not. In her pageant she sets herself to comprehend both history and the present moment, her audience and its natural environment—nothing less, in fact, than life in itself and in its wholeness, so far as it can be grasped by someone actually involved in it at a given point in time and place and society. In consequence art, as she represents it, does not simply affirm art. Instead it has its function as an intrinsic activity of human living: the artist is in life, not standing outside and above it. Her pageant is strikingly not a perfected work of art, and the novel itself hardly strives for aesthetic perfection as such. This lack of aesthetic finish, which is a response to the texture of life as it is actually known and experienced, marks an immensely difficult and valuable achievement. It represents Virginia Woolf's acceptance of life such as it is in a degree exceeding that of *The Waves*, which though it affirmed such an acceptance remained very self-consciously involved in its art. In *Between the Acts* she went her furthest towards that ultimate subordination of the interests of art to the interests of life which constitutes the maturity of the imagination.

It will be observed that this maturity meant an immense advance upon *The Years*. There is none of the hysteria of the isolated and alienated literary mind. There is instead a remarkable serenity of mood, remarkable because the mind can contemplate the full extent of human folly and failure, and at the same time enter fully and sympathetically into the lives of individuals. The point might be illustrated by the obvious contrasts between the wounded caricaturing of the Victorian social system in *The Years*, and the detached humour with which the same material is treated in the pageant. The signal distinction of the novel, in fact, is that while there is an acutely discriminating intelligence at work in the prose, lucidly discovering and evaluating the varieties of human behaviour, there is beyond that, and comprehending whatever it discovers, an urbane and poised mind disposed to accept and to participate in all that makes up human life. This constitutes a maturity far surpassing the aesthetic maturity of *To the Lighthouse*, and crowning the labours of *The Waves* and *The Years*. . . .

From Chapter 6 of *Virginia Woolf*, Oliver and Boyd, Edinburgh and London, 1963, pp. 84–6.

MARILYN ZORN

The Pageant in *Between the Acts*

... The dramatic, and in this case rhetorical, device of the Pageant is recognition. One says rhetorical because the Pageant is a spirited and oftentimes gay parody of the contents of a course in 'Survey of English Literature'. ...

The whole Pageant, indeed the whole novel, is built on this series of echoes and half-echoes from Shakespeare, Shelley, Byron, and Tennyson. Meant to be conveyed is all of English literature from the nursery rhyme to a passage of Isa's which rings clearly of T. S. Eliot: 'All's equal there. Unblowing, ungrowing are the roses there. Change is not; nor the mutable and lovable ... where hand seeks hand and eye seeks shelter from eye' (pp. 181–2). This kind of allusion is the central device of style in the novel. It is as if the author willed that her audience find a traditional body of myth in the evocation of a traditional literature.

For it is not until recognition occurs that communal feeling may spring into being. One need only list the incidents wherein dramatic recognition occurs in the Pageant to establish the importance of the device for the Pageant and, duplicating the Pageant, for its audience as well. Art here simplifies and sharpens the experience of recognition; for Isa and Giles, Bart and Lucy, and the others, life is more complex than it would appear to be when the Prince and Carinthia recognize one another and fall in love. ' "It was enough. Enough. Enough," Isa repeated. All else was verbiage, repetition' (p. 110). Yet certainly we are meant to see the parallelism between that scene and the flash of memory we are given of Giles's meeting with Isa. Time, of course, adds the gentleman in grey and Mrs Manresa to the lives of the lovers who met, fishing for salmon. The eighteenth-century comedy is built on a series of mistaken identities and motives, but the end is accomplished and love finds its way when Flavinda and Valentine confront the two aged intriguers with the realization of their folly and the recognition of true love. About the Victorians, Miss La Trobe is not quite so optimistic. Mr Budge doesn't recognize the difference between guarding the law and trespassing on the domain of the private soul, between righteousness and self-righteousness. Presumably he cannot see his own hypocrisy. Having hooded their motives from each other, the Victorians have hooded them from themselves.

All of which brings the audience to the essential scene of recognition in the play. The final scene is no pageant. The author merely brings forward a line of mirrors and catches her audience's flatly self-conscious pose of themselves. Nor can the audience ignore the presence of the image. Each must fix his face, affronted by his own reflection, before he can afford recognition of himself or of his neighbour. Thus there can be no meeting, except perhaps a meeting of masks. Few of them dare be even so honest as to make the mirror offered a means toward fixing the outer face, as does Mrs Manresa.

What Virginia Woolf implies throughout her artificially and deliberately contrived pageant is that no relationship—poetic, rhetorical, or real—between humans is possible without a recognition of the essential soul as distinct from the roles it must play. Recognition and the refusal to recognize the human being for what he is occur throughout the novel as well as the play. Identities are confused and obliterated. Isa's lack of understanding of Giles and his of her are symbolized by Isa's imagining adultery with the gentleman in grey and Giles's actual affair with Manresa (Lust). Giles cannot realize that William Dodge is a human being in need of sympathy because he sees only the mask of William's homosexuality. Bart (aptly named by Mrs Woolf by the Tereus/Procne relationship with Lucy—'Swallow, my sister, O sister Swallow'), on the other hand, commits a daily rape upon Lucy's sensibilities (his delight in excoriating her religion) and upon little George because he cannot recognize the sanctity of their souls. To Lucy is given the most exquisite and sensitive sympathies of any of them, and even though she cannot remember William Dodge's name, she instinctively knows his difficulty and pities him—does not only pity, but can give him love:

> 'I'm William,' he interrupted.
> At that she smiled a ravishing girl's smile, as if the wind had warmed the wintry blue in her eyes to amber.... And he wished to kneel before her, to kiss her hand, and to say ... but you've healed me (pp. 89–90).

Recognition can lead to reconciliation if it is whole and selfless and honest. This seems to be what Mrs Woolf is saying. And it is not surprising that this is what the 'gifted lady', Miss La Trobe, is saying to her audience as well. After the Pageant is ended, the anonymous voice affirms to the audience:

> Before we part, ladies and gentlemen, before we go ... let's talk in words of one syllable, without larding, stuffing or cant. Let's break the rhythm and forget the rhyme. And calmly consider ourselves. Ourselves. Some bony. Some fat.... Liars most of us, thieves too....
> All the same.... There's something to be said: for our kindness to the cat; note too in today's paper 'Dearly loved by his wife'; and the impulse which leads us—mark you, when no one's looking—to the window at midnight to smell the bean. Or the resolute refusal

of some pimpled dirty little scrub in sandals to sell his soul . . . (pp. 218-9).

And then begins the 'right' piece—'was it Bach, Handel, Beethoven, Mozart or nobody famous, but merely some traditional tune?' (p. 220) —which brings the audience together for the final moment of reconciliation with the scraps, orts and fragments of self and neighbour. A moment of vision, if we are to believe Mrs Woolf, which justifies the vague longings of the human heart for beauty and serenity, undisturbed by the life of 'Monday or Tuesday'.

What . . . Message? Only that Mrs Woolf inundated *Between the Acts* with the rarest and finest thing she knew—her affirmation of the artist's vision, his great gift to the individual and to society: to hold up for one timeless moment the mirror of Reality and catch there the human soul, creating by the radiance of that vision—Harmony.

From Marilyn Zorn, 'The Pageant in *Between the Acts*', *Modern Fiction Studies*, Vol. 2, 1956, pp. 31-5 (33-5).

MARJORIE BRACE

Worshipping Solid Objects

... The serious writers of the twenties were very conscious of living in an age of transition, bereft of any desirable order of values; very aware of living breathlessly in motion, in time, without roots. Psychologically speaking, they had no home for quiet living. Alone and unsupported on an unfathomable journey, their personal lives were as if confined to hotel rooms. They were spectators in every sense, observing not only other people, but themselves, with that traveller's eye which perceives nothing but gesture. Emotions—and, above all, relations with others—were seen through lighted windows as dramatic postures, and so became false. To 'understand' the human character became more and more impossible, not through ignorance or superficiality or love for mystery, but because on that disintegrating journey in which no fixed standard of judgment could endure, it was absolutely what was *unknowable*.

To Virginia Woolf the unknowableness of people and the impossibilities of communion were never, as to some of her contemporaries, comic or ironic or of intellectual interest, but terrifying. The devices others used for evading genuine characterization, the 'scientific' analyses, the violent caricatures, the self-conscious satirical melancholy posturing, all these were repulsive to her serious and lyrical nature. That responsiveness to what was truly alive which, in her literary essays, emerged in such tender appreciations of personalities from a warmer past, left her shivering but determined before the cold looming problems of her own time. Like one of the insects she loved to describe, we see her progressing erratically through her novels, feeling, as with painfully sensitive antennae along a chilly wall, for some new approach to the mystery. With each novel, the characters become more shadowy and we have in their stead, almost alarmingly real—as large as life and twice as natural—seasons, boats, oceans, leaves, furniture; the very streams of consciousness, when not a highly lyrical poetry, sound like overheard conversations or the confessions a stranger might impart on a train. And in *A Haunted House*, her collected short stories,—some of them left unrevised at her death, some, even in final form, mere sketches—there is a kind of unity the novels, for all their elaboration, never achieved: the traveller's view has perhaps never been expressed with such purity, in all its supervividness of seeing and hearing, its rocket-like bursts of excitement, its flat returns to the hotel room of the self.

Here is a reiterated motif of human departure from the haunted 'houses' of the past:

> They wanted to leave this house because they wanted to change their style of furniture, so he said . . . very interesting people because one will never see them again, never know what happened next . . . we were torn asunder, as one is torn from the old lady about to pour out tea and the young man about to hit the tennis ball in the back garden of the suburban villa as one rushes past in the train. . . . Why, if one wants to compare life to anything it is being blown through the Tube at fifty miles an hour, with one's hair flying back like the tail of a race-horse.

Reality is something glimpsed as one tears past, something arrested, timeless; is a flower-stalk or the old lady about to pour tea.

But the old lady lives only in a picture. She is not 'understood', she has no capacity for action other than to complete a gesture, and she fades like a landscape from our sight, her living and dying of obviously less significance to a traveller than the decay of her house or garden. This world in which old ladies may be equivalent in value to the weather or snails on a rock, while unquestionably it has uncovered new areas of awareness, has also brought fresh terror to individual experience, beside which the spectator's joy is seen dwindling to a nervous, transient release. In such a story as 'An Unwritten Novel' the narrator, observing a tragic face on a train, invents a withered spinster's life story to suit it, only to have the fancy exploded when the 'character' is met at the station by a son. And what is the reaction? 'Well, my world's done for! What do I stand on? What do I know? Who am I? Life's bare as a bone.' But almost at once (still aboard the train and not back in the hotel room) the last look 'flooded her anew. Mysterious figures! Who are you! Where tonight will you sleep? . . . unknown figures, you I adore; if I open my arms it's you I embrace —adorable world!'

The note of hysteria is unmistakable: the traveller's intoxicating sense of illegitimate freedom is darkened by inevitable returns to a somehow equally spurious 'reality', subjective as well as objective, where, alone and looking at himself, he is compelled to dissolve his *own* capacity for action by self-mockery: 'I wish I could hit upon a pleasant track of thought, indirectly reflecting credit on myself. . . . Dressing up the figure of myself in my own mind, stealthily, not openly adoring it, for if I did that I should catch myself out. . . .'

Virginia Woolf is least interesting when, defending, as it were, this powerless condition, she presents as the only possible foil the stock culprit of so many novels of the period: the ignoble person who has not the grace to realize his own self-imprisonment. Such are the humanitarians in 'The Man Who Loved His Kind' who, anxious to prove their own way of loving humanity to be the only right one, end up by hating everybody. Similarly, there is the girl in 'The New Dress' whose costume, designed to be exotic, appears only laughably eccentric to her once she arrives at a party where she is doomed to be either snubbed or bored because—we grasp the point only too quickly—her own unreflecting egotism turns all dresses and parties drab. We have met this girl too often before. We have been informed by too many writers that we *are* that girl, that, always taking ourselves to parties, we miss the thrills of observation through a lighted window.

We do not question the Baudelairian horrors of existence so poisoned by subjectivity that even the ocean speaks '*un langage connu*'. What we do question is the finality of the either-or implication. Is it not just this artificial pendulum-swing between human falseness and an inhuman world of 'mysterious figures' that adulterates such writing with a morally dubious quality? Is it not just as untenable and, even, smug, to be forever appreciative of our 'honesty' and thrilled with the unknown?

Virginia Woolf's work never resolved this issue, but when it was confronted, as in her story 'Solid Objects', she created some of the most remarkable symbolic expressions of our time. Here is John, standing for Parliament—that is all we are told about him—who one day at the beach finds a lump of green glass so mysteriously significant that he begins hunting everywhere for similar objects for his mantel. 'They were useful,' Virginia Woolf tells us slyly, 'for a man upon the brink of a brilliant career has any number of papers to keep in order—addresses to constituents, declarations of policy, appeals for subscriptions. . . .' Soon he finds a fragment of china so extraordinary that he misses a meeting trying to fish it from an obscure recess.

> Set opposite the lump of glass it looked a creature from another world—freakish and fantastic as a harlequin. The contrast between the china so vivid and alert, and the glass so mute and contemplative, fascinated him.

He begins to haunt wasteland, rubbish heaps, demolished houses, neglects everything in the search, and the day he is not elected finds him elate, for he has discovered

> a most remarkable piece of iron, massy and globular, but so cold and heavy, so black and metallic, that it was evidently alien to the earth and had its origin in one of the dead stars or was itself the cinder of a moon. And yet it stood upon the same ledge with the lump of glass and the star-shaped china.

In this apparent negation of all human values, we find a partial and —in its very inadequacy—a desperate, almost noble attempt to reinvoke them on some unapproached plane. The documents, leading articles, cabinet ministers—that reality which made Virginia Woolf exclaim, 'The military sound of the word is enough!'—these things had become so profoundly inimical to the interests of the other, inner reality (in turn horrified by its own isolation) that the two realities cancelled each other out. There was nothing but to establish entirely new relations as, waking from a nightmare, 'one turns on the light and lies worshipping the chest of drawers, worshipping solidity, worshipping the impersonal world which is a proof of some existence other than ours. That is what one must be sure of.'

An excess of moral sensibility and humaneness caused Virginia Woolf to move into an inhuman and morally irresponsible world, making her write of insects, trees, old boards and broken china as if they were inhabited in an ancient sense by gods and spirits. She was trying to shift perspective, to start all over again, by creating in the unconscious some life-giving pagan emotion which, roving through the detritus of civilization, might also move into relation with a chemical, mineral, biological, fourth-dimensional universe, and so toward a new morality.

The virtue of the spectator's view is that, tearing down houses and disrupting dead relationships, it helps this fresh start. Its defect is that no matter how great the artist's moral anxiety and sensibility, it makes quite hopeless those human relations the difficulty of which sent him on his travels at the beginning. That is why, in almost all the novelists of the transitional group, definite or memorable characters are sacrificed to the qualities of things which should be distinct from literature, such as psychology, or music or painting. But the truth of a psychological analysis, the significance in a musical theme or a picture is complete and not, as great literature is, implicit with potential action. More successfully than any prose writer of her time, Virginia Woolf was, with words, a musician and a painter. What she was not can be seen in comparison with the few who, working with her material and intention, were not dazzled by a new conception of time, but lived densely within it; who placed human beings in new relations with each other as well as with the physical world.

This is so of Proust, whose wealth of colour and object is not seen through a window, for all its brilliance, but crowds upon us; through all the subtle change and mingling of his novel the great characters seem to flower amid the trees and founder majestically among the decaying houses and documents. And if Proust introduced new meanings for time and space, Joyce entered a new moral dimension. In his utter dispersion of the elements of character and his reintegration of them in the unique figure of Bloom, Joyce suggested a possible humanization of those complex and desolating perceptions which depopulated the world of Virginia Woolf of all but ghosts and drove her toward a pagan reanimation of objects.

But it is she who seems closer to us now, and prophetic. The martial sound of reality and the clashes of malformed egos have invaded the landscape as well as the midnight room with cold ferocity. We are reminded as we read her that journeys now have grimmer purposes, that the traveller no longer stops at those marvellous way-stations, those heavenly côte d'Azurs she explored so exquisitely. The general motivation of current fiction recalls those base persons whose lack of self-knowledge she repudiated with fastidious disgust. If we cavil at her writing like a painter, how are we to endure those novelists whose work, under such an analogy, could only be compared with some curious Landseer school, populated with people like vicious or noble dogs? Who do not even comprehend the questions left unanswered by a previous literary generation? To be surrounded with what is dying, and to know it, is better than to mistake death for life.

From this perspective we look back at Leopold Bloom standing as on some distant peak, the last fully human man in literature. We cannot help, as we open Virginia Woolf's books, climbing on her train with something of her own desperate joy. Despite our completed knowledge of the life bare as a bone at the journey's end, the rushing air is so alive, so cold and salty with the sea, so warm with flowering vines; and there is also the amazing piece of iron, solid and concentrated, to hold like a talisman in our hands.

From 'Worshipping Solid Objects: The Pagan World of Virginia Woolf', *Accent*, Vol. 4, 1944, pp. 246–51 (247–51).

Select Bibliography

THE WORKS OF VIRGINIA WOOLF

The Uniform Edition of Virginia Woolf's novels is published in London by The Hogarth Press, which was founded by the Woolfs in 1917. Harcourt, Brace and Company are her publishers in the United States, but the important Preface written in 1928 for *Mrs Dalloway* is printed in the Modern Library Edition published by Random House, New York.

During her lifetime Virginia Woolf collected only two volumes of her essays: *The Common Reader* (1925); *The Common Reader: Second Series* (1932). However, since her death in 1941 further essays have been published in a number of volumes and these have now been regrouped in the four-volume *Collected Essays* (1966–7). For a student of her novels the most interesting essays (with date of first publication) are: 'Modern Fiction' (1919); 'On Re-reading Novels' (1922); 'Mr Bennett and Mrs Brown' (1923); 'Notes on an Elizabethan Play' (1925); 'The Narrow Bridge of Art' (1927).

Penguin Books have issued most of the novels and some non-fiction in paperback.

BIBLIOGRAPHY

A Bibliography of Virginia Woolf, compiled by B. J. Kirkpatrick and first published in London in 1957 by Rupert Hart-Davis, was revised and reissued in 1967. It is a very useful guide, especially to the uncollected reviews, articles and stories written by Virginia Woolf.

BIOGRAPHY

There has been no adequate biography of Virginia Woolf, though Professor Quentin Bell, her nephew, is preparing an authorized life. The chief value of Aileen Pippett's *The Moth and the Star*, published in the United States in 1955, is that it quotes extensively from the correspondence of Virginia Woolf and Victoria Sackville-West. A very important source for those who wish to discover more about the life and personality of Virginia Woolf is *A Writer's Diary*, The Hogarth Press, 1953. This absorbing volume contains Leonard Woolf's selection from the twenty-eight large notebooks containing Virginia Woolf's diary and is the indispensable guide to her mind and her art as a novelist. Leonard Woolf's autobiography has been published by The Hogarth Press: *Sowing* (1960); *Growing* (1961); *Beginning Again* (1964); *Downhill All the Way* (1967); *The Journey Not the Arrival Matters* (1969). Two good background studies are Quentin Bell's *Bloomsbury*, Weidenfeld and Nicolson, London, 1968, short, witty and delightfully illustrated, and J. K. Johnstone's *The Bloomsbury Group*, Secker and Warburg, London, 1954, which is more philosophical and literary.

CRITICAL STUDIES

(a) *Books*

Of the score of studies of Virginia Woolf's novels the best are:

A. D. Moody: *Virginia Woolf*, Oliver and Boyd, Edinburgh and London, 1963. (The last chapter answers the *Scrutiny* attack on the novels.)
Josephine O'Brien Schaefer: *The Three-fold Nature of Reality in the Novels of Virginia Woolf*, Mouton and Co., The Hague, 1965.
Another important work is Jean Guiguet's *Virginia Woolf and Her Works*, The Hogarth Press, 1965. It makes good use of *A Writer's Diary* and has the most thorough and up-to-date bibliography of books and articles on Virginia Woolf.

(b) *Articles and Chapters in General Works* (*excluding* those selected for this volume)

E. Auerbach: Chapter 20 of *Mimesis*, Doubleday Anchor Book, New York, 1957.
Reuben A. Brower: Chapter 7 of *The Fields of Light*, Oxford University Press, New York, 1962, pp. 123–37. (Key words and ideas in *Mrs Dalloway*.)
Dean Doner: 'Virginia Woolf: the Service of Style', *Modern Fiction Studies*, Vol. 2, 1956, pp. 1–12. (*Jacob's Room* and *Mrs Dalloway*.)
M. Goldman: 'Virginia Woolf as Critic and Reader', *P.M.L.A.*, Vol. 80, 1965, pp. 275–84. (Favourable assessment of V.W.'s achievement as a critic.)
P. and M. Havard-Williams: 'Perceptive Contemplation in the Work of Virginia Woolf', *English Studies*, Vol. 35, 1954, pp. 97–116.
C. G. Hoffman: 'From Short Story to Novel: the Manuscript Revisions of Virginia Woolf's *Mrs Dalloway*', *Modern Fiction Studies*, Vol. 14, 1968, pp. 171–86. (Shows conclusively that the 'first version' of *Mrs D.* to which V.W. refers in her Preface was never actually written.)
R. Humphrey: *Stream of Consciousness Technique in the Modern Novel*, University of California Press, Berkeley and Los Angeles, 1954, *passim*.
S. Hynes: 'The Whole Contention between Mr Bennett and Mrs Woolf', *Novel*, Vol. 1, 1967, pp. 34–44. (A full account of the controversy referred to in my Introduction.)
F. R. Leavis: 'After *To the Lighthouse*', *Scrutiny*, Vol. 10, 1942, pp. 295–8. (The source of the passage quoted in my Introduction.)
G. Pedersen: 'Vision in *To the Lighthouse*', *P.M.L.A.*, Vol. 73, 1958, pp. 585–600. (Mrs Ramsay a monster of egotism.)
I. Rantavaara: 'On Romantic Imagery in Virginia Woolf's *The Waves*', *Neuphilologische Mitteilungen*, Vol. 60, 1959, pp. 72–89. (Discusses the sea imagery and identifies Rhoda's 'poem about a hedge' as Shelley's 'The Question'.)